Don't *Sabotage* Your Success!

Make Office Politics Work

By Karen Ginsburg Wood

Enlightened Concepts Publishing
OAKLAND, CALIFORNIA

First printing 2001

ISBN 0-9702143-0-8

LCCN 00-134667

ATTENTION CORPORATIONS, UNIVERSITIES, COLLEGES, AND PROFESSIONAL ORGANIZATIONS: Quantity discounts are available on bulk purchases of this book for educational purposes. Special books or book excerpts can also be created to fit specific needs. For information, please contact Enlightened Concepts Publishing, P.O. Box 1017, Oakland, CA 94604-1017; to place an order call 800-266-5564.

This book is dedicated to all those who have suffered and shared their stories so I might learn and pass the benefits on to you, the reader and student.

My family has been supportive and loving as I began to realize this is what I was put on the earth to do. And my husband has been a gift I could never reciprocate. He is kind, supportive, and patient, and has inspired me to become the best. Thank you, my darling, for all those times you pushed me out of my comfort zone and kept me thinking positive thoughts when I began to lose faith. You are my miracle.

I like to think my career mishaps have not been in vain so I can pass along the dirty details to you, the reader. Many of the people who suffered along the way, however, would likely feel differently about revealing their mistakes. Therefore, I have shielded everyone I love and care about and have changed every name except for that of my husband. He is already used to my talking about his experiences and has forgiven me long ago.

~ CONTENTS ~

*You must do the thing
you think you cannot do.*

Eleanor Roosevelt (1884–1962), American stateswoman

I graduated in the top of my class from the number one business logistics program in the country. I had a 4.0 in my major when I graduated from Penn State. The biggest corporations came to recruit me. I selected a position in logistics at an eleven-billion-dollar-plus international conglomerate.

After six months of working, I was in the middle of what was then considered the world's largest leveraged buyout in history. The company announced there would be cutbacks, a wage freeze, and no promotions. That was my signal to leave. I worked too hard and was too ambitious to be slowed down so early in my career. I moved out west to California after accepting a job with another top-consumer products company.

The work I did was excellent and my reviews reflected it, but I always felt like I had to fight for every promotion I got. It was a mystery I could be adding so much value in my roles and yet not really getting the recognition I thought I deserved.

Were my standards too high? Was I with the wrong people who just could not appreciate my special talents?

The years passed. Eventually, I became aware of a male coworker, Louis, who had the equivalent on paper of my education and experience. I thought, however, my education and previous work experience were stronger. It just so happened Louis took over many of the projects I launched. I would start the project from an idea, implement it, run it as a program, and turn the reins over to him. Each time this occurred, the peers I had worked with on those programs would tell me how poor a performer Louis was.

This information blew me away because management was moving Louis pretty quickly in his career. Soon, he passed me in promotions. He truly was the golden boy.

Now I began to wonder what the hell was going on. I had been so successful in school. I had the pick of any job when I got out. The results were excellent on every project I had worked on. I surpassed goals, came in under budget, increased sales, and met time lines. I developed significant relationships in other departments that didn't even exist before my tenure. These relationships became the basis for my projects succeeding and also won me respect from my peers.

I began to wonder if my slow progression was because I was a female.

I hated that this could even be an option. My generation didn't believe there were differences between female and male roles. I thought I could be a firefighter or a ballerina, or both. It was my choice. Now for the first time in my life, I began to consider maybe there *was* some bias in the work place.

One day at the copier, I noticed someone had left the salary figures for the entire department there. What a find! I took this information and began to compare myself to my peers. What I discovered would change my life. There it was, in black and white: Louis was being compensated more than me by over 25 percent!

Now that I had proof we were being treated differently, I needed to leave. I realized I would never fit into this environment. I told myself, it's *them.*

I went to graduate school and earned a degree in corporate finance. I secured a software modeling job, which paid more than double my previous salary, and became my first six-figure position. I felt like I was back on track to becoming the cream of the crop. Soon, I would be experiencing much success and happiness.

After the first month, I was starting to have some minor complaints. Probably the worst of it all was the travel. Even though the trip was only forty-five miles from my house, it took anywhere from one and one-half to two hours, each way. On top of that, I flew every week to another city—Portland, Los Angeles, Chicago.

After the second month, I was becoming pretty cranky about the travel and working conditions. My office space was a coffee table and a side chair in my boss' office. My job was to model distribution networks on the software. My equipment broke every ergonomic rule, and I was in physical pain at the end of each twelve-hour day.

I would come home after a grueling day at the office and a couple hours on the road to my loving husband. I was always angry when I got home and my husband would always be doing something that would make me want to yell at him. For instance, whether he greeted me at the door or didn't, I was angry. I was very unhappy.

By the third month, I realized I needed to take control of the situation. I thought maybe it would be better if I could work out of my house instead of schlepping all the way down to Santa

Clara. I proposed the idea to my boss and he agreed. *Great!* I thought. *Things are getting better already!*

At the end of the third month, my boss and I had set up a Wednesday meeting to informally review some software modeling I was doing. Wednesday morning I decided I just couldn't bear the thought of traveling into the office, carrying all that heavy computer equipment, and working at the coffee table. I called to tell him I wanted to reschedule our meeting for Friday.

He didn't want to reschedule and again asked me to come in that day. I finally blurted out *No! I will come in on Friday.* To which he responded, *Okay. I guess I'll see you on Friday.*

Friday came. I still remember the chill in the air and the pouring rain. I got into my car, reset the odometer, and began the long commute from Alameda to Santa Clara.

I arrived at my company's building and found a covered spot in the parking garage. I recalled the conversation I had with my husband the night before. I told him I could not tolerate the working conditions at my job and I had to start making some demands. I was going to take charge of my career. If they wouldn't accommodate me, I'd just quit. Yeah.

Yeah, right. I had never quit any job in my life. Especially not a six-figure-salary job.

I shook the rain out of my umbrella and took off my coat. My boss called me into his office. Great! And he seemed to be in a good mood!

He said there was a call for me, but as I began to reach for the phone, he moved the speaker to the center of his desk. I was a little confused but went along with it. The woman's voice on the speakerphone introduced herself as so-and-so from human resources. I remember feeling pretty good at that moment. And then she told me I was terminated.

My boss—or rather, my ex-boss—reached over to the fax machine and pulled off a fresh fax that bullet-pointed the details of my dismissal.

Within ten minutes it was over. I remember shaking hands with my ex-boss, smiling, and saying, "I hope and wish you the best success. It's too bad it didn't work out."

I went down to the lobby of the building and called my husband. "Guess what, honey."

"You quit today?"

"Noooooooooo."

"You got fired today?"

"Yeeeeeeeeeeees." He asked if I was okay. I told him I thought I was. But I was devastated. This was my first six-figure job and I had gotten fired after just three months. I was still in the training phase!

That incident changed me forever. It forced me to take a serious look at myself. I looked back over my career and I began to realize this was *not* the first time I had experienced failure.

After five years at my previous company, I resigned to go back to school and finish my graduate degree in corporate finance. When I left, no one cared. Five years and no relationships to show for it. I mean, I had friendships with peers, wonderful relationships I still have today. But, in terms of managers who wanted to keep me on their team, there was no one. The fact there were no managers eager to keep me after five years of excellent performance was a great failure on my part.

Sophia Loren said mistakes are the dues one pays for a full life. And I was just beginning to realize I had lived quite a full life.

This has been a long journey for me but the good news is I have discovered some hopeful insights along the way that have helped me to create the success and happiness I enjoy today.

First, the male-female thing was a bit of a copout for me. It was easy to point to that as the reason for my misery and lack of opportunity because when I looked up in the organization all I saw were men. However, when I went back and examined the situation I was reminded there were also some women who had achieved a high status. That very fact gave me hope there was some formula for getting to where they got.

In addition, I also discovered there were men who did not move up. This was an important fact because it held some clue that perhaps there was something that was necessary and it appeared to be independent of sex. That is, if some women could succeed and some men could fail or at least be held back, then perhaps the game was actually unbiased after all.

The second thing I learned is that this is a very difficult self-discovery process. I became quite depressed as I began to uncover the mistakes in my career. At the time I didn't know I was doing anything wrong—it was only in hindsight my foibles seemed so obvious. I didn't have the luxury of having a book or workshop to help me understand what behavior works and what behavior doesn't work. So it was by trial and error—and more errors—that I happened upon the dynamics of relationships in the work place. Each time I uncovered a significant principle of relationships it was like a million light bulbs going off in my head: "Oh, no! I can't believe I did that!"

Third, I discovered the real meaning of happiness and success.

When I was in college, I had a group of girlfriends who were a lot of fun to be with. Every weekend we went to various parties. It just so happened that some of these parties would be wildly fun, with great music, lots of cute guys wanting to talk to us, and good beer. Some of the parties would be pretty boring with no music, people sitting around talking, and maybe the worst beer you ever drank.

It didn't seem to matter whether I was at a fun party or a boring party, I always had a good time if I was with my friends. So, I used to say, it's not where you are but who you're with that determines if you're having a good time. And that's true today. Some days you might love the work you do and some days you might be bored to death, but if you enjoy great relationships in your work place, you'll enjoy what you do. Therefore, good relationships are important for happiness.

Success is something I've tried to define over the years and I feel like I've knocked this one out. Success is more than just money and status, I know, because I've had both and the feeling of success was fleeting.

Success is the feeling that your work is valued and more importantly that you are valued in the organization. You are given opportunities to develop and stretch. You are picked to be on teams based on your outstanding reputation. People want to work with you. You can make mistakes and you know you will be protected. Everyone makes mistakes in their careers and you have confidence that in making them you won't be out on the street looking for a new job.

Success is the flexibility to modify your job as your personal life changes. When my husband and I wanted to have a baby, I went to my boss and told him I needed to stop traveling for a year. His response was to ask what the company needed to do to keep me there. In summary, the relationship you develop with your boss is key to your feeling and becoming successful. Therefore, good relationships are important for success.

The surprising conclusion from this analysis and self-discovery has been that the relationships in the organization are critical to creating success and happiness. Why was this such a surprise for me? Because somewhere along the way I was raised to believe I could be successful based on the excellent quality of my work. I thought people would point to me and say I was successful because I'm really good at what I do. Favors? Relationships? Reciprocity? Asking for help? Oh my goodness, no—that didn't even enter my mind.

My analysis began with a closer look at the dynamics of the relationship between manager and subordinate. I began down the road of discovering the principles for developing strong relationships with my superiors because I could see this indeed was the key to achieving happiness and success in my career.

I wrote this book because I wanted to pass on the knowledge that saved me from a life of misery, frustration, and disappointment. I created a workshop based on the principles in this book because I wanted to get feedback from real people on how this affected their lives.

The response has been incredible. People from every phase in their careers to every level in business have come to me for guidance. They say this information has changed their lives. This knowledge has changed my life. I pass it on to you with the hope you may benefit. I wish you all the success and happiness you endeavor to create.

~ APPROACH ~

The approach of how I teach is a little bit different from most of the books that have been written on success.

When I started reading books on this subject, most had the same format: Here are a bunch of very successful people. Let's look at their characteristics and figure out what makes them successful. The idea is if you know what makes someone successful, all you have to do is assume those traits and you too can be successful.

Although I believe there is merit to that formula, it doesn't always work. Even if you do almost everything the successful people do, it doesn't help you identify habits and behaviors that are sabotaging your success.

Other books can identify behaviors that could get you in trouble but give you no clue as to the correct behavior. In other words, if I know that by doing something I will actually alienate myself from the people I am trying to connect with, perhaps I could stop doing whatever it is I am doing, but how do I still reach my original goal? Most of our behavior and actions in the work place are rooted in some type of objective we are trying to accomplish. Therefore, if we stop certain sabotaging behaviors, we need to know the correct behaviors to replace them with so we can still be effective in meeting our original objective.

What I was looking for was a way to understand what I was doing wrong, why it was getting me into trouble, and I needed some strategies to help meet my originally intended objective.

The way this book has been designed is to deliver the principles in a way you can understand:

- What behaviors are sabotaging your success.
- Why those behaviors have negative consequences.
- Strategies for you to meet your originally intended objective.

In addition, you'll learn the dynamics of work place relationships, which will enable you to:

- Build a strong relationship with your boss.
- Understand what you have a right to expect in the relationship.
- Understand the key signs when a relationship is failing.
- Build strong relationships with your subordinates.
- Understand when it's time to move on.
- Leverage your equity in the relationships you've built.

The bottom line is you will now have the control and the knowledge to manage your career so you can have all the happiness and success you wish.

As I said before, pain accompanies the self-discovery of mistakes that have been made. Therefore, I have provided a meditation to clear the mind and begin the journey.

Forgive others for hurting you and remember to forgive yourself. Accept and see others they way they are and accept yourself, warts and all. Practice nonjudgment of others and seek to understand yourself. Believe you are perfect and that you are learning how to increase your capacity for success and happiness. Believe everything is working for your ultimate good, and lessons are waiting to be discovered. Someone in your life loves you, so you are loved. Above all, you are love.

Now you are ready to begin the journey.

*You will do foolish things,
but do them with
enthusiasm.*

Colette (1873–1954), French writer

One of the first major lessons I got in the "real world" after leaving the safe confines of higher learning was realizing much of what I learned in school was wrong, if not severely detrimental to my career. Remember back in school how if you got the right answer you were rewarded? In fact, *that's* what mattered. You didn't *have to* schmooze the teacher to get good grades. You didn't have to invest in the relationship. You didn't have to worry about your social skills. Social skills were generally developed and displayed by hanging out with friends, our peers.

Many of the peers we interacted with, both male and female, were able to benefit from our ability to excel. In other words, we could tutor our friends in the subjects we understood well. This was the source of positive experiences, bonding, and satisfaction in helping others make it through school. Sometimes we might have even stayed up all night just debating different concepts we had learned that day. Remember the time when learning was encouraged and *fun and exciting?*

And remember those teachers who *loved* to be challenged with our difficult questions? Yeah, they probably even invited a debate or two in class just to help us understand the complexity of the issues they were presenting. And those in the class who actively participated in those discussions got rewarded and those who didn't might have even *lost* credit. That's how we learned and we were rewarded for it with positive reinforcement. In other words, we were *conditioned* that it was pleasurable to get the right answer or if we couldn't get the right answer we should do our damnedest to show we at least *wanted* to get the right answer by asking lots of questions.

That was then but this is now. Today in the work place you may be producing a high-quality work product (that is, getting the right answers), and yet you don't seem to be getting the level of reward you expect. The recognition is not what it used to be. Imagine a long list of performers in your department with their appropriate contributions posted like some list after midterms. You eagerly approach the list looking...looking...ah, there is your name and you got 96 percent. Wake up! The whole process just got very subjective. It's very different in this world. We were not well prepared for this type of evaluation.

You begin to find that asking hard questions often alienates you from the very people with whom you seek to connect. Debating an issue does not draw any of the fun and excitement it used to; it often ends up in frustration and alienation. What is going on here? Did I miss something in school?

What we have here is a culture within the business world that influences the way people behave and make decisions.

Most importantly, this culture helps to support the existing power structures in the organization. Because this culture is virtually invisible, it is difficult to detect and consequently difficult to change or influence.

When I was researching this subject, I happened upon a study that had been done in the 1980s by Kotter and Heskett in their book *Corporate Culture and Performance*. Kotter and Heskett were trying to identify what kind of corporate cultures produced strong long-term financial success.

They were able to identify cultures with strong positive and strong negative characteristics. The strong positive cultures were the ones that had long-term financial success, while the strong negative cultures lagged. At first, I thought these must be two entirely different types of companies. Later, I began to realize both of these cultures exist simultaneously in any company. Different perspectives could be possible depending on whom you asked the question: Is this a good place to work?

Kotter and Heskett described the negative characteristics they observed: managers displayed arrogance and are discouraged from looking outside of the company/department to solve problems. Managers had little regard for employees. The culture became belligerent to change.

Let's use an analogy to explain the point. Suppose you could choose between two vacations. On the first vacation, the weather is beautiful every day, the hotel is fabulous, and the food is delicious. On the second vacation, the weather is dreary, the hotel is austere, and the food is plain. Which would you pick?

What if I said that on the first vacation you have to go with the person you get along with least? On the second vacation you get to take your soul mate. I'm guessing you would now choose the second vacation.

The point is that the experience will be perceived by many factors but most importantly, by your state of mind and your interactions with the people around you. If you have favorable conditions but bad relations, you probably won't remember the experience well. However, if you have unfavorable conditions but excellent relations, you might be able to laugh off and even enjoy the unfavorable conditions and remember the experience positively.

This is true in companies. Two people can work in the same company, even in the same department, and have entirely different perceptions of whether or not they are valued, happy, and successful.

Kotter and Heskett further explain that the main purpose of behaviors in the negative cultures is to support the political structures within them. Does this mean that political structures only exist in negative cultures? We'd like to think so! But the truth is hierarchical organizations produce political structures. It's simply a byproduct of power and influence. Microsoft is one of the best companies in the world to work for and for many years has had an amazing long-term financial track record. However, even Microsoft has political structures. Things get done through political structures. Another way of saying it is that someone has to be responsible for meeting the end goal and that is a person with some degree of power and influence.

Cultures are perceived negatively by the individuals who are not able to thrive in them. These individuals do not understand how to get things done through the political structures. There is little or no coaching by more experienced employees to guide the newer ones. And so the company can become a very cold and unsatisfying place to work.

The key to success and happiness is to understand the dynamics of political structures. More specifically, to understand the relationships within the hierarchical organization. The three types of relationships—subordinates, peers, and superiors—are different and need to be treated differently.

The culture incentive system is actually set up to discourage us from displaying qualities or characteristics that are not in alignment with the culture, and reward or benefit us when we display qualities or characteristics that are in alignment with the culture. Many of the ways we are encouraged or discouraged are very subtle, which explains why it takes so many years to "figure this culture thing out."

Many people have stated that when women and other minorities reach a predetermined critical mass at high levels in Corporate America, the culture will change and become more "feminine." My strong belief is the culture will not change. The reason being that women and other minorities who succeeded did so because they learned or knew how to fit in the current culture. It's a culture they understand and in which they are successful. So, why the heck would they change it?

As I expanded my research to include both men and women, I learned both sexes have some success in these cultures and both have failures. I seem to gravitate more toward understanding the failures. I find hope in seeing failure applied evenly to both sexes. And so there is hope for us all!

Make no mistake—the road to happiness and success in most business cultures is *not* obvious to most of us. This is not well laid out for us in any education we might have received in school. What you might find as you read this book is some of these "lessons" may contradict everything you have understood up to this point to be valid on how to be successful. I encourage you to challenge yourself as you read on and ask yourself what you have got to lose? Especially if what you are doing now is *not* working, what have you got to lose?

My attitude is positive in delivering the messages in this book.

In the following pages, I will teach you many of the hard lessons I have personally experienced. These lessons became the principles for this book. I am living proof that these principles can build a career of success and happiness. Learn it and live it. You deserve all the happiness and all the success you endeavor to create.

CHAPTER ONE

Don't Act Like That!

If you have made
mistakes…there is always
another chance for you
…you may have a fresh
start any moment you
choose, for this thing we
call "failure" is not the
falling down, but the
staying down.

Mary Pickford (1893–1979), American actress

This is one of the most important chapters in the entire book. In consulting we refer to this chapter as building the business case.

Maybe at this point you have gotten a couple of not-so-great reviews, or you're not very pleased where you are at this point in your career. In spite of this, you're not convinced your actions have directly contributed to your situation.

Maybe you are just too smart for the corporate world. Maybe you should work for yourself, since no one really seems to understand your unique value. These were all the things I said to myself many times. I couldn't believe the frustration I was experiencing in my career was my own doing.

You Are in Good Company

The one thing that has truly amazed me is the diverse cross-section of professionals who have come to me for help. Lawyers, vice presidents, doctors, graduates, scientists, accountants, buyers, people working in small high-tech startups, people working in large established corporations, young people, people who have been working decades, men, and women.

What is the common thread in all these different types of people? Number one, they are all smart. In fact, many are overachievers, like myself. Number two, they all know they are smart. That second sentence is key because this is where a strength can become a fatal flaw.

The fact that you know you are smart can boost your confidence and spur you along in your career. Inner confidence helps you take risks, pushes you to continue to challenge yourself and stay abreast of the changes in your industry.

On the other hand, knowing you are smart, even more so than others, can make you arrogant, blowing up your ego. Without realizing it, your knowledge is used as a way to put others in their place, to reinforce your superiority. Finally, you feel isolated. You are the only one who truly understands what is going on (in the department) and you have the great misfortune of working with a bunch of morons. What would they do without you?

Are You Seeing Yourself the Way Others See You?

The first exercise in uncovering what's happening here is to review the negative or constructive characteristics that have been ascribed to you over the years. This could have come directly from a superior or even indirectly from peers and subordinates. This could have been in a written or formal evaluation or some kind of feedback or coaching session Please be advised the importance of this process. It is not necessary for you to agree with any of the negative feedback that has been provided. Trust me, it will all make sense as we proceed.

You might find it helpful to make a list of the negative characteristics that have been ascribed to you. People in my workshops are usually amazed with the list and what it means. Since I've been running this workshop for a while now, I can share lots of characteristics with you. Maybe you'll see some with which you can connect.

Category one
- Works too much
- Efficient
- Pit bull
- Excellent credentials
- Works too much to stop to think
- Too serious about work
- Too conscientious about work
- Too smart
- Takes on too much work
- Tactical
- Direct
- Intense
- Not following chain of command
- Professional
- Unprofessional/passionate

- Too focused on work
- Perfectionist
- Too honest
- Doesn't ask for help
- Independent
- Controlling

Hey, I didn't mean that!

These characteristics are actual examples from people just like you and me. What should strike you about these particular characteristics is that by definition they should be seen as *positive*. For instance, isn't it a good thing to be professional, focused, and efficient? What about passionate? I related to that one right away. I thought that's what leaders were looking for—people who were passionate about their beliefs. How is it that being focused on getting the job done, doing it well, and not stopping for chitchat has gotten us, well, into trouble?

Early on in my career, I had been assigned a small project, dubbed by management as a transportation program. My department was handed a slip of paper from the sales department with various expected sales for U.S. cities. My responsibility was to coordinate the shipment of product from plants to warehouses based on the slip of paper from sales.

The problem, as management laid out, was that once we deployed inventory to warehouses to support the sales numbers, we ended up redeploying product all over the United States. So, in effect, we had huge transportation variances. The biggest culprits were the Los Angeles and New York markets. We'd deploy thousands of cases to a Los Angeles warehouse only to have to turn around and ship those cases to the New York warehouse to support a heavier-than-expected demand in the Northeast.

Since I had a logistics education, my inclination was to look at this transportation problem from a planning perspective. In addition, I ran reports and began to analyze previous sales patterns across the country to gain better insights as to how this product sold throughout the different markets. I began building relationships in marketing, sales, and manufacturing. I posed the idea of a cross-functional planning session. All agreed to attend.

At the first planning session, I remember asking the marketing person how the sales forecast was developed. The reports I had run on last year's sales were very different from the current plan we were discussing. The marketing person looked up from her forecast and said these were the numbers from last year. Again I looked at my report and didn't see how this forecast reflected what we actually sold. I asked, "Is this what we sold last year?" and she replied, "No, this is what we forecasted last year."

At that point someone responded, "Oh, that's not good." I chimed in that I had run a report that detailed what we actually shipped to stores last year and maybe we could use that as a starting point. The group agreed and so began one of the most successful planning models in the company's history.

The results were fantastic. Customer service greatly improved. We cut down redeployment because we had better sales information on where the product would actually sell. In our efforts to have the right product in the right place at the right time, the planning team agreed we needed to build certain inventories higher than other inventories for several logistical reasons, like lead times and demand.

The peers on my team liked me. I developed several friendships—one that has lasted almost ten years. It seemed obvious any performance review for my work on this project should be excellent. Maybe I would even get promoted.

I will never forget my review for this project. We had just had a reorganization and I was working for a new manager. This manager only knew me by reputation and had not personally managed me over the course of the year I was working as an inventory planner.

As I said, the results from the customer service side were excellent, however, there was a big setback to the plant managers who were responsible for the inventory levels. The Los Angeles and Cleveland plant managers were unhappy with their new and higher inventory levels. This level made sense: If we lowered it, we would be forced to either miss customer shipments or expedite more expensive transportation of the product to the warehouses. This was better for the company overall, but worse for the Los Angeles and Cleveland plant managers who now appeared to be doing a poorer job managing their inventory levels.

My new manager came from the manufacturing side of the organization. More specifically, he came from the plants themselves. He understood and empathized with the plant managers' daily dilemmas. Needless to say, when he reviewed my accomplishments, he did so through the plant managers' eyes.

My manager said , "Karen, you are getting things accomplished, but you are like a *pit bull*, and you won't stop until you reach your objective." Hey, wait a minute, I thought that was the point—to accomplish the stated objective?! Pit bull? Where did that come from? I was not considered mean—I had made friends with all the people I worked closely with (peers). Also, people would frequently ask me for help and to join their project teams. I don't believe they would have confused me with a pit bull. Anyway, the overall review was barely satisfactory due to the negative situation that had been created at two plants. The fact that customer service and the transportation variance had greatly improved did not seem to be relevant.

This was actually the first red flag something was wrong in my relationship with my superior. The very fact that my well-meaning intentions to do a good job were interpreted negatively meant something was amiss. Looking back at the list, if you too can identify with characteristics that have been ascribed to you in a negative way, you are having problems in your relationship with your boss. This is the first post in the business case.

Does this mean we can never exhibit these types of behaviors and be perceived as positive? No. Everything is style and context.

First, we've established that the context you are operating in is a poor relationship. You are having some problems with your superior because even your well-intended behaviors are being seen as negative.

Second, your style could perhaps be what has created an atmosphere of distrust with your boss.

I want to be clear that I am not advocating a "yes-sir" attitude. There would be little joy in just being agreeable and going with the flow. This would be a very short book if the main idea was how to say yes. Instead, you will learn that by securing the relationship with your boss, you can act independently, be passionate about ideas, get the job done, and be seen as a rising star.

Another program I developed and managed required the removal of millions of dollars of obsolete inventory out of the company. I worked with cross-functional groups like marketing, sales, logistics, and finance. We exceeded our sales goal by 400 percent for the year! Pretty impressive? My management, who was not a big fan of mine for more reasons I will disclose as we proceed, decided to "ask around" and see how I was doing, even though the results certainly spoke for themselves.

The results were positive. All of the people I worked with (peers) agreed I had improved things. After all, we had collectively found a profitable way to move expensive inventory out of the company. Management came back and said to me at my review, "Well, you appear to be doing a good job, Karen. We asked the other departments you were involved with and no one had anything bad to say." I guess by default they had to acknowledge I was doing a good job.

This was so incredibly frustrating to me at the time. This was also another red flag that my management was not in my corner. Even though I was getting results beyond the targets they had set, they still felt like they were "stuck" with me.

What was I doing wrong? At this early point in my career I was only beginning to understand that results are *secondary*. This was very confusing. It was the total opposite of everything I had learned and been conditioned to do up until this point in my life. I came from a black-and-white perspective. Things are either good or bad, you are either right or wrong. Everything could be quantified. I exceed goals and expectations; why didn't that translate into promotions and pats on the back from management. Obviously, the results were not primary. So what the hell was *primary?*

Remember the guy, Louis, I mentioned earlier? By studying him I began to uncover the mysteries of the work place.

He was favorably looked at as "The Golden Boy," meaning management felt he was going to do a good job, no matter what they gave him. When I learned Louis was *not* performing anywhere near what management was rewarding him, I was so frustrated! And then I was angry! Finally, I had to ask, "What is going on here? Is management on drugs?" I decided management was probably not on drugs, so I began to collude with some of my female peers. And the pieces of the puzzle began to fall into place.

Upper management adored Louis. He had developed wonderful relationships with his managers. They were willing to promote him and pay him more money—in spite of the fact his work quality was adequate or poor. The truth is, I had not developed relationships with anyone beyond my level or so. I was courteous to everyone and respectful to my managers. I tried to do everything they expected from me with complete enthusiasm and surpass their expectations. But I failed to develop any meaningful relationships with any managers in the department. Later on in my career this would become my mission. I wanted to understand how to develop strong positive relationships with upper management.

Now take a look at the second category of characteristics ascribed to people by their bosses:

Second category

- Hard to get along with
- Defensive
- Doesn't have confidence in me
- Poor communicator
- Nonconfrontational
- Not seen as a leader
- Harsh
- Unfriendly
- Cold
- Too quiet
- Not known personally
- Aggressive
- Passive-aggressive

- Defensive
- Reserved
- Poor communication skills
- Too short with others
- Difficult
- Abrasive
- Anti-social
- Don't care enough
- Internalize too much
- Unapproachable

Now you've really pissed me off!

What is the likely outcome when all of our best and well-intended efforts are misinterpreted as negative? If you said "utter frustration," you are correct. Look at this second list. It's a culmination of all the frustration we've experienced because we have been misunderstood. We begin to pull back, withdraw, and eventually shut down. Whether we are aware of it or not, we are in a cycle of pain and unhappiness.

This is the second post of the business case. This last point establishes we are now suffering because of our poor relationships.

What I have learned throughout my career is just how important the relationship with my boss was. In fact, that relationship can be the key to success and happiness. I never would have believed that early on in my career. I really believed my work would speak for itself and I would be rewarded on the merits of my excellent work product. I paid little attention to cultivating relationships with my superiors. To tell the truth, they made me a little uncomfortable, even nervous.

Think about this. Your manager/boss can give you the reassurance your work is valued. But more importantly that *you* are valued within the organization. Your boss has the power to groom you and provide you with opportunities for advancement. This relationship is actually quite critical to you feeling secure and valued and ultimately being happy and successful in your job.

Let's take a look at sports to demonstrate a point. Remember when the Dallas Cowboys were one of the weakest teams in football? Jerry Jones, the owner of the Cowboys, fired the then-coach, Tom Landry, to bring in the highly successful Miami University college football coach, Jimmy Johnson. Let's revisit the aftermath of the parting of ways between Jimmy Johnson, the former coach of the Dallas Cowboys, and Jerry Jones, the owner.

When Coach Johnson started, the Cowboys' record was nothing to write home about: Year one coaching the Cowboys yielded a 1 and 15 record and the second year 7 and 9. Eventually, Coach Johnson got the Cowboys to the Super Bowl and won—two years in a row!

So what happened? It appears from many articles published on the topic Coach Johnson wanted control. He said, "Without question [Jones] wanted to be more involved, and I'm accustomed to doing things a certain way. And so that's where it ended up being a problem."[1]

Jones and Coach Johnson had a public and private falling out. Coach Johnson stated publicly he was considering leaving the Cowboys and Jones responded back to the press that he is the only one who determines if Coach Johnson should stay or leave. Jones appeared to attack Coach Johnson more and more in the media and Johnson responded accordingly. Needless to say, there seemed to be a mutual agreement to get Coach Johnson out and within one day his successor, Barry Switzer, was hired and Johnson's remaining five-year contract was null and void.

Before Switzer accepted the coaching position, he asked Jerry Jones the greatest single question, which summed up in a nutshell the utter illogic of the situation. "Would you or Jimmy please explain to me how two guys could be on top of the world and win two straight Super Bowls and not be able to get along with each other?"[2]

There are a lot more insights into the falling out of Jimmy Johnson and Jerry Jones we will explore in later chapters. The point here is that the results you deliver, no matter how good, are *secondary* to your ability to work well with your managers.

The Moral of This Chapter

There is a very important moral or bottom line to all we have learned about ourselves at this point. No one wants to pick anyone who falls into any of the previous lists of characteristics to be on his or her team. Think about this: Would you rather pick someone you knew you could trust to work on your team, someone who would be loyal, or someone who was really smart who could do the job but was a big pain in the neck to work with and on top of that thought he or she was smarter than you? Even Jerry Jones would rather pick a loyal subject like Switzer who was unknown in pro football than the proven (but disloyal) Jimmy Johnson. Life is short, nothing is rocket science in the world of business. And 99.9 percent of the time you end up picking people you like and trust.

As I've grown in my ability to understand and master relationships in the work place, I can honestly say I am a different person today than I was when I started in my career. Because of my knowledge of relationships, I feel lucky I've been able to carve out a successful career for myself. But being the glutton for punishment I am, I thought it would be interesting to go back to some of managers I worked for when

I was just starting out and see if they would like me better now.

As it turned out, I found out an old manager—who actually liked me—was returning back to the company where I had worked for him almost five years previously. I called him and we met for lunch.

At that point in my career, I had reached a point where I was thinking about a change. I had been a traveling consultant for more than two years and my husband was telling me we could not continue to live like that anymore. I was considering other opportunities.

At lunch with my old boss, we talked about old times. He talked a lot about his last job, how he made a lot of money, lost respect for his boss, and eventually was asked to leave. He was on the phone with an old manager from our old company. When he told the manager he was losing his job, the manager offered him a position in the old department. Isn't it awesome how relationships can get you picked?

During lunch I dropped a million hints I was considering other opportunities besides consulting. Not once did my old boss as much as offer me the name of someone in the company who was hiring. I was saddened by the fact that even after five years, this manager still saw a lot of my negative characteristics and would not pick me or even recommend me to be on a team. Even though I had changed, it didn't matter because this manager based our relationship on my old behavior.

I just saw the film *Contact* for the fifth time. In the movie, Jodie Foster, a very serious scientist, discovers a message from a distant star, Vega. The message is translated and reveals instructions on how to build a machine that could transport its passengers to another place in the universe. It becomes a global undertaking and soon every country wants to be involved in some way. A committee is formed to select the perfect representative to go on the trip. Jodie Foster's character is frustrated because she thinks she should go since she discovered the message. Her character is interesting in that she breaks a lot of rules of relationship principles. In the final selection, she is not chosen. Rather, the most politically astute senior male candidate is chosen. He is very likable. He tells the committee what they need to hear to feel he has their best interests at heart, he is like them, and that he will be loyal to the objective of the mission.

Jodie Foster's character isn't loyal to anyone but herself and her own objectives. In a way you admire her for being so passionate about her ideas. But I couldn't help but wonder if she could have secured more trust in her relationships, she might have been less frustrated in her career. She is belligerent to anyone who is above her in the hierarchical structure of the government programs. Her smarts have made her quite arrogant.

The only one who is superior to her in power and influence who takes a chance on her is some mythical eccentric scientist. He likes her and paves the way for her to realize her career goals. Unfortunately for us, this guy seldom exists in any of our careers. Most of the people we work for are just regular people who are looking to build their teams with people they can trust.

I relate this concept to my workshop students and one of the participants tells me of a story where his boss was interviewing candidates. The age-old question, "What do you see yourself doing in five years?" comes up, and the candidate responds with confidence and enthusiasm, "I want your job!"

Think about what this means: You can't trust me because I'm out for myself and looking to hoist you out of the job you have. Only in Hollywood does this work out for the candidate.

Every relationship requires trust to grow. Trust is a building block for the critical relationships you seek to forge. Almost everything you do or have done to sabotage your success has been rooted in destroying trust. Therefore, we will now begin to explore what common behaviors destroy trust and the strategies to employ trust-building behaviors.

There are many types of relationships in our lives, but we are going to focus on relationships in the business place. The principles of business relationships are quite different from other relationships in your life, mainly because work place relationships are hierarchical in nature. There is a certain etiquette that goes along with being a subordinate, a peer, and a superior.

So, in order for you to understand trust-building and trust-destroying behavior, it must be explained in the context of these hierarchical relationships.

One final note. For the next chapters we will discuss behavior with an assumption that you want to connect with your superior's vision. In chapter three, there is a section entitled "But what if I don't agree with my manager's vision?" that will discuss considerations when you cannot support your boss. I want to be very clear that I would never advocate a good soldier approach to relationships, which dictates you keep your mouth shut and follow the orders of someone you have no respect for. I want to move you into happiness and success, which means a rich dynamic relationship with people you respect.

CHAPTER TWO

Don't Act Like Your Mother!

⋘⋙

*We can do no great
things—only small things
with great love.*

Mother Teresa (1910–1997), founder, Missionaries of Charity

⋘⋙

I loved the title of this section because it really addresses the familiarity we have with certain behaviors because we've been around them and are used to them in our personal lives. By the way, when I discovered this, I had no children, so you needn't be a mother or even female to experience this behavior firsthand.

Don't Tell Everyone What To Do!

Remember when you were growing up how your mother (or someone else's mother) had that incredibly annoying habit of telling us what we *should*:

"Why don't you cut your hair? You have such a nice face."

"Why don't you wear your hair long? Boys like long hair."

"Did you remember to clean your room?"

"Why don't you clean up your room? You haven't seen the floor in days."

"You really shouldn't eat that, you *certainly* don't need it."

Do those statements give you goose bumps? What amazes me is I have witnessed people in business use that same condescending tone to make suggestions to coworkers, or worse, to their superiors. I don't care if your manager's mother still talks to him like that, or even his wife for that matter. No one better treat him in that manner at work.

We have to be very careful here because there may even be a tendency for us to carry this annoying trait into out personal lives, such as the way we sometimes talk to our spouses, children, and other family members. Therefore, it is a style we are comfortable with and may find natural to bring into the work place. Notice how benign some of those sentences seem. Most of them *appear* to be suggestions or even inquiries.

In the book, *You Just Don't Understand*, Dr. Tannen explains that the message a woman gives to a man when helping is, "This is good for you," but the message may be instead received by the man as, "I am more competent than you."[3] That is, the woman is verbalizing she is one up on the man. In other words, by offering help you could be telling someone they are subordinate to you.

This behavior may be rooted in some kind of superiority complex we have over the other person, maybe because of our experience or knowledge of the particular situation at hand. That's why mothers can be so effective at this. They are in a position of higher authority, they have more experience and knowledge about a situation, and they want desperately to change our behavior—for our own good, of course.

Therefore, what may start out as a genuine intention to impart knowledge may end up as a power struggle in who is the dominant one. And if the person you are struggling with is a superior, you may even be perceived as insubordinate and not respecting your position in the hierarchy.

Most people extol this behavior without even realizing it. In my workshop, I ask students to think of specific examples where they have done this. It's not easy and because this is one of the first exercises, most people aren't ready to open up. Since most people learn by example, I ask the class to concentrate on any example, not necessarily themselves.

Chelsea was a manager in the accounting department for a small and rapidly growing coffee company. She could not think of any examples where she had made the mistake of telling her boss what to do so she deferred to something a coworker had done.

Later, Chelsea came up at one of the breaks and asked my advice on a matter that concerned her and the CEO of her company. He was speaking at a Town Hall meeting for the small company and at the end asked if there were any questions.

Chelsea was smart and had noticed there had been an explosion of food companies infiltrating the airports as well as the airlines themselves. You could now order a Starbucks coffee with a Happy Meal on your flight from San Francisco to Chicago. Chelsea raised her hand and asked, "What is our company doing to take advantage of the airport market?"

The CEO's response was explosive. In front of everyone he exclaimed the current strategy of the company was very focused. He became defensive. Chelsea was bewildered.

Without realizing it, she had sabotaged herself by actually asking a question in such a way that it was more of a command or directive than an innocent question. The question, as she put it, implied the company *should* already have a strategy and if they didn't they should put one together.

It's also probably true that Chelsea is very insightful. And maybe the CEO was getting tired of the Wall Street analysts telling him he should have a strategy for penetrating the airport market. Chelsea became an easy target for his built-up frustration.

I pointed this out to Chelsea as we analyzed what happened and her reaction was disbelief. She had never intended to tell the CEO how to do his job. She admired him and wanted to secure a relationship with him while the company was small. She sincerely thought she was helping things along by asking a simple question in the meeting. She wanted to show him she was engaged and interested in the company's growth.

Later that week, Chelsea became more aware of her communication style toward others and noticed she had a habit of telling people what to do. It really amazed her because she had been convinced she was a good manager, a loyal worker, and a strong communicator.

Remember what I told you before in the Preface? It gets kind of depressing when you realize you've been doing something wrong and never intended to. Be patient, we've got a way to go yet.

Please take a moment if you haven't already to take an inventory of incidents where you might have told your boss what to do. This is how you will learn and have the control not to repeat your mistake. Someone once said, the mistake is not in making the mistake but in repeating it.

I know I said we've got to separate our personal relationships from our business relationships because they are different, but I have a good personal story that clearly demonstrates the point of this principle.

In my relationship with my husband, I consider myself part of a team. We both agree that I am the more analytical one and so I sometimes feel it is my duty to point out what obviously needs to get done so we may proceed with our plans.

For instance, if we need to be somewhere by two o'clock, I'll say, "Honey, could you feed and walk the dogs? Are you done? Could you empty the trash? Are you busy? Could you diaper the baby? Put your shoes on, I'm almost ready."

By the time we are ready to walk out the door, he is so angry at me we almost always get into a fight. What happened? I thought we were working as team? I was bathing the baby while he was walking the dogs. I was showering while he was diapering the baby. What's the problem?

He tells me he feels he's been bossed around, told what to do like he was my subordinate. I told him I was just pointing out the next steps in the logistics to get out the door in time.

The bottom line is, it feels so natural to ask someone to do what you think is obviously beneficial to the team or the company. Be careful, even in an established relationship where you have trust this can easily be misinterpreted. Your peers will think you are being condescending and your boss will consider you insubordinate.

In summary, when you behave in a way that someone interprets as telling him or her what to do, you are sending the message that you are superior and that the other person needs your help. The result is almost always a power struggle, since the other person is looking to re-establish his peer or superior relationship status with you.

Don't Help Everyone With Everything!

One never notices
what has been done;
one can only see what
remains to be done.

Marie Curie (1867–1934), French scientist

Here is another annoying habit dear old sweet Mom taught us. Since Mom was more experienced at sewing, cooking, laundry, etc., she sometimes took it upon herself to help everyone out in the family. Poor Mom, she barely had time for herself. And remember how resentful she would sometimes get? She really didn't like it and eventually complained that all the responsibilities were *dumped* on her.

The truth is, I don't know why Mom did that. But I do know this can be a highly destructive and unsatisfying quality for us in the work place.

People usually demonstrate this behavior by volunteering or being volunteered for many responsibilities. The problem develops when a sense of resentment begins to brew. This resentment will eat at your sincerity and eventually you will no longer be perceived as a team player on anyone's team except your own. You will be viewed as selfish and high maintenance, that is, requiring too much attention. That label is practically the kiss of death in business. No one wants an uncommitted high-maintenance person on his or her team.

Doing Too Much Versus Just Being Manipulative

There are other relationship implications of "doing too much." A friend of mine, Pamela, was traveling with her immediate supervisor, a woman, and also another high-ranking manager, a man. Since Pamela arrived at the airport ahead of the other two, she thought it would be helpful to check in for everyone in the party. In addition to minimizing check-in time, they would all be seated next to each other. When the male superior learned of Pamela's actions, he became furious, commenting, "I've been with you nearly all day. Why would I want to sit with you on the plane as well!" Pamela was completely surprised as to the negative degree of this superior's reaction. Clearly, Pamela had only intended to save him time checking-in and guarantee him a better seat in the process. She was confused how such intentions could result in this kind of backlash.

Just like when Mom used to try to do things for us we wanted to do ourselves, we find ourselves getting frustrated if others do things for us that we feel are our own responsibility. In the case of many men (and women), it can even be interpreted as *manipulative*. When you take away the option for someone to turn down your offer, you have literally forced them to do what you want, regardless of your true intentions.

A good rule of thumb when dealing with this type of situation, is to remember people deserve the freedom to chose what they wish to do or not, no matter how trivial it may seem to you. An offer to expedite would almost never be looked at negatively, unless of course, it is not an offer but an announcement of what you have already performed. I always remind myself that everyone has the right to do things slowly, inefficiently, and even make mistakes. Unless there is a strong safety reason, you should avoid intervention unless invited. I have found this to be quite successful in dealing better with managers, friends, husbands, sisters, and brothers.

Another situation occurs when we feel *obligated* to pick up responsibility no one else will take. This should usually be a red flag to you. When I was working on an inventory deployment program, I determined that an analysis of the previous year's promotion was required before our team could plan the current year's promotions. Seems very logical, right? Well, as it turned out marketing, or sales, or manufacturing did not have ready access to that type of data. I had excellent programming skills and could develop programs to extract the data that was required to successfully run the inventory planning meetings. Marketing, sales, and manufacturing were supportive of my valuable contribution to the team.

However, my managers were not. When they learned of the additional efforts I was going to in order to plan inventory, they verbalized their disapproval. I can still remember my manager telling me, "I don't see why you provide that kind of information for the team. That's the responsibility of marketing or manufacturing to come up with that analysis, not our department's." And I tried to explain that marketing and manufacturing lacked the skills and resources to develop the programs I was able to create. Since it was a *team* effort, I continued, it didn't really matter *who* did *what*, as long as we could reach our objective. And finally, I didn't *mind* putting in the extra effort, after all, the team valued it and I found it rather easy to perform. There should have been a big red flag going off in my head, but I was destined to learn the hard way.

At the end of my first year in the role of inventory planner, my peers were unbelievably supportive. The woman I worked with in marketing wanted to recruit me into her department! The product was more available and more efficiently transported around the country. There had been real measurable improvements since I began working with the inventory planning program. As I mentioned earlier, however, there were some who were negatively impacted by the program. In order to improve product availability on the West Coast, we agreed as a team the inventory levels would have to increase in the West Coast distribution centers. Well, guess what happened? The West Coast distribution center manager was pissed off because his inventories increased but he was still held responsible for lower inventory levels. The net impact was that this manager, along with a couple of others, were negatively impacted by the program.

When it came time for my evaluation, my manager did not speak to marketing, sales, or manufacturing. Instead, he went to the West Coast distribution center manager for feedback. He asked him if he was better off as a result of the program. Well, even though the program made the company better off, the West Coast distribution center manager was *worse off.*

What ended up happening is I received one of the worst reviews of my career. The language was critical and harsh. The feedback solicited for my review all supported the conclusion I was not best managing my time and my internal customers were worse off.

After I rolled out of that assignment, I transitioned it to another manager. At the first inventory planning meeting, he explained he would not be providing the detailed product sales analysis I had in the past. The manufacturing person was livid and actually started screaming at my replacement. After some negotiation, he acquiesced to provide some historical sales trends but only temporarily. Eventually, he stopped providing it altogether.

This manager was very successful in the department. He received promotions, recognition, visibility, and money. What is the bottom line here? In order to advance in the organization, you must value your time. If you don't, you probably will not be seen as promotional material. What is a little bit confusing, though, is sometimes what we think is a valuable use of our time is not valued by management. Therefore, be open to feedback and make adjustments as necessary. If you can't persuade management you are making valuable use of your time, minimize or eliminate those efforts. They may get you well liked among your peers, but they will leave you out of favor with your manager.

Another good example comes to mind about the pitfalls of taking on too much. A very successful woman I know, Margaret, complained she wished some of the women she works with would be more consistent in their commitments. Margaret is a pink-Cadillac-driving beauty consultant for Mary Kay Cosmetics. She boasts over sixty consultants in her unit and some nine hundred clients! This is a woman who knows how to become successful.

Recently, Margaret was looking toward the future. She is a Director who wants to become a National, which will help her retire early in ten years. In order to become a National, Margaret needs to have a certain number of people trained in selling the product line. She told me she just didn't see how she was going to make that happen because of small things that were eating up a lot of her time.

She told me the story of a beauty consultant who had entered the business about a year ago after borrowing money from Margaret to finance her showcase and inventory. In addition, this consultant made personal requests for time and/or product, which would regularly interrupt Margaret's weekly meetings that focused on training new consultants. Margaret felt very sorry for this woman and wanted to give her the attention and nurturing she needed so she could develop, but at the same time Margaret felt resentful this woman was not matching Margaret's efforts.

First of all, Margaret valued her time equally. In other words, the time she spent training new consultants was equal to time spent with an inconsiderate consultant who had not demonstrated consistency in her business. If Margaret has a vision of becoming a National and to do that needs to train so many people per year, it should follow that Margaret's most valuable use of time should be training new consultants.

Second of all, Margaret valued all opportunities the same. This is a mistake I saw my husband make early in his career. As a self-employed plaintiff's lawyer, my husband Albert receives his payment, or share, from the settlement. It would seem more cases equals more shares equals more money. But that is not correct because some cases are much more difficult than others, some are more risky than others, and some have smaller potential payouts than others. Therefore, all cases are not the same.

I sat down with my husband and we identified some of the criteria necessary to value a potential case. Now, he uses that criteria to determine if he should accept a case or drop a case, should factors of the case change. That's really important because decisions you make today are always based on some underlying assumptions. These assumptions are more than likely to change in the future, therefore, it is wise to continually monitor and evaluate situations.

The justification for evaluating cases is simple: If Albert chooses to help everyone (a noble effort), he may run himself out of business, which means in the long run he won't be able to help anyone. Therefore, if Albert wants to help as many people as possible, it is in his and *the client's* best interests to help only those clients who meet a set of criteria. There is some flexibility, here, of course. By managing the business more successfully today, Albert has the luxury to help *some* people who fall outside of the general criteria. The result is he can take on some pro bono work for people who wouldn't be able to afford his time, and he feels good knowing he can make a difference and still have a thriving business.

Getting back to Margaret, the Mary Kay Director, I told her to look at her situation from a bigger perspective. First,

Margaret has committed to her husband that she will become a National so they can enjoy their retirement in the next ten years. Second, Margaret has a commitment to the new consultants coming in to develop them into profitable independents. But Margaret knows very well not all new consultants are the same. Some are more committed than others, some have more sales potential than others, and so on. Therefore, based on criteria of what makes a good potential beauty consultant, Margaret should focus more of her efforts on those women who have the highest chance of success. The consultants with medium potential could be delegated to some of the other more seasoned consultants. That way Margaret can free up more of her time to focus on the women with the greatest potential payoff, and other consultants can benefit from learning some management skills. And finally, those women who fail to meet any of the listed criteria should receive little to no attention after a predetermined time. The justification is simple: If Margaret has to spend most of her time attending to consultants who produce the lowest results, her *entire* unit is negatively impacted in the short run, and in the long run she will not meet her objective.

This is an important concept to grasp. I see many of us getting caught up in the details of things, lives, people, which can actually *prevent* us from moving to the next step. We mix satisfying characteristics of personal relationships with business. It is enjoyable to connect and help people in our personal lives, but in business it can be detrimental. Remember, the more successful you become, the more impact and influence you will have, which means the *more* people you will be able to help.

Margaret cited at the beginning of our discussion she felt she was too nice and needed some assertiveness training. Be very careful here. Untempered assertiveness is a negative characteristic—it got me fired. In this particular instance, what is required is a shift in paradigm, or a new way of thinking. That is, the old way of viewing her time was that Margaret has to help everyone. The new way of thinking is that Margaret puts her time where she gets the most benefit, delegates when possible, and lays down rules for new consultants coming in so they understand if they don't contribute a certain amount of effort, they will not receive much support.

We have talked about why you would want to minimize an additional workload. Here are some ideas on how to do just that.

First, if you are truly loaded down with work, avoid opportunities to increase your responsibilities. Keep a low profile, delegate whenever possible. The only one who can manage your workload is you.

Second, avoid the tendency to voluntarily pick up more responsibilities. Like Mom, we love to be needed. The more we do, the more needed we must be, *right?* Wrong. I don't care if you do the work of ten men, if you leave, the company will quickly replace you. Mom was lucky because there was only one Mom, but we are commodities in the work place. Therefore, if you have an unsatisfied need to be needed, I recommend you adopt a pet or do volunteer work, but do not take on a high workload.

Make more time rather than responsibilities. This allows time for relationship building, something I never made time for early on in my career. I didn't have time to "socialize" with anyone because I was trying to impress my manager by showing him what an efficient machine I was. In fact, I along with most of my career-struggling counterparts did more work on average than the "Golden Boys." And it so followed the "Golden Boys" had more time to informally interact with managers in the department. My peers and I, consequently, would phone each other at night to complain about how much socializing and brown-nosing was going on and how it was amazing anything got done in that department.

Relationship building is so important we will spend an entire chapter just dedicated to it. The main concept I want to leave you with is this: More responsibilities does not equal better performance and higher recognition. Therefore, be very selective at what you choose to add to your workload.

Don't Correct Others in Public!

We don't see things as they are, we see them as we are.

Anaïs Nin (1903–1977), French-born American writer

This one should bring back scary memories if your mother demonstrated this behavior at all. I guess if we had to conclude what the motivation was, it would be (on some level) the desire to help others *improve* themselves. Things mothers would urge us to do include: "Sit up straight, you're slouching," or "You can't order that, you're on a diet,"or "You're allergic to that, don't go near that."

The point is this: No matter how well intending Mom was with her dispensing of advice and friendly reminders, it definitely rubbed most of us the wrong way. We wanted to be grown up already and able to act and think independently and even make mistakes! At least they were our mistakes. Mom was probably only trying to insulate us from what she knew would be a path of discomfort, pain, or worse.

Many of us continue to use this strategy in the work place with only the best of intentions. What we are actually doing is annoying the hell out of the people we work for (or with) and alienating us from the very people we are trying to help.

Carried to an extreme, some of us may publicly correct behavior. Have you heard the term "saving face"? It means you give the person with whom you are conversing the opportunity to keep his or her dignity and pride. In other words, don't ever act or say something that will cause someone else to feel inferior, embarrassed, or humiliated. By correcting someone in public, you further magnify the humiliation of the moment.

Correcting others in public is one of the most significant sabotaging behaviors because it does a couple of things. First, you don't allow the other person to save face, which forces them into a power struggle with you as they attempt to regain their hierarchical standing. Second, it shows you are out for yourself and you don't care about them. In other words, you are disloyal. You have destroyed trust. This behavior will keep you from moving forward and can even result in getting you fired.

A friend of my husband, another lawyer, was contemplating taking my workshop. She called me to talk about the content of what I taught. Eventually, I began to focus on her and what event(s) led up to her inquiry about the workshop.

She was a lawyer for a prominent bank. There was a very high level meeting in which her boss and several other vice presidents were discussing a business matter. In the middle of the conversation, she interrupted her boss and corrected him. Right there in front of his superiors and peers. Her intention? To restate the correct facts. The result? She was fired.

My ex-boss, Ralph, told me a similar story. He worked in a small and fast growing startup company. He was having a painful time working with his boss, who had become increasingly unethical as the business got more difficult.

At a meeting that included the CEO and president (Ralph's boss), some other vice presidents, and Ralph, Ralph openly and publicly corrected his despised boss. No matter that his boss was wrong; in the next scene, his boss was recommending to the CEO that Ralph be terminated. Ralph went back to his office and realized he had dug his own grave. Maybe in an effort to escape from the situation he couldn't or wouldn't quit, he did what he did knowing it would result in his departure.

So what happens if you really do need to correct your manager on a major point he made in front of a whole bunch of people? This situation actually happened at starkly different points in my career.

Early in my career, I was managing packaging materials for a cookie that wasn't selling so well. Marketing had told me they would be phasing out the current packaging in favor of some better packaging that would encourage more sales for the cookie. So I went back to my desk and cranked out the material plan for the new product launch. I was very thorough. I estimated how much material I would have to throw away and how much of this new stuff I would have to order. I didn't discuss the information with anyone nor did anyone approach me.

There was a big meeting during which management would make a decision on the new packaging for this cookie. I was probably the lowest level person at this meeting, which also included my manager, my manager's boss (the vice president), plus high-ranking people from other departments like marketing, sales, and finance. Other products were discussed and finally my cookie was the center of attention. Marketing was pushing for launching into the new packaging material as soon as possible and began to discuss the type of marketing strategy that would be used to roll out the improved cookie. I must have decided that was my cue, so I cut in with "for a March roll out, we would have approximately $1,000,000 worth of old printed material which would be unusable in the new form and cannot be returned to the supplier, since it was printed...." I remember hearing my manager choking in the background and someone else saying something like, "Whoa!"

Before I could say another word, the vice president of my department interrupted me and said something about us getting back to marketing at a later date with the *correct* numbers, to which the marketing vice president interrupted that we may need to re-look at the timing of any launch this year if our liability was so high in materials, to which the sales vice president interrupted and asked, somewhat rhetorically, how could our inventories be so high on materials? He began to insinuate my department (and of course I) must have dropped the ball by ordering the wrong quantity of materials. I couldn't believe what was happening. I did my homework and was ready for the meeting. I had the right answers. Everyone was pissed off. *And I didn't end up being the hero I thought I would be.*

Do you understand what was happening at this meeting? I had inadvertently subordinated everyone there because I had information that could influence the entire course of a marketing decision. Therefore, the vice president *began to symbolically knock me down back into my subordinate role.* I had disrupted the hierarchical dynamic. Even more interesting was that my department, logistics, was a support department for marketing. Therefore, I had also subordinated the entire marketing department since they would have to change their course based on my department's information that I had announced. This explains why my vice president was quick to note that we would get back to marketing with the "correct numbers." He was trying to symbolically acknowledge that this was marketing's decision and his department would support—*not* direct.

Somewhere in the middle to later point in my career, I realized my errors from the past and was extremely conscientious of correcting any superior, *ever.* As I began a new role in consulting, I worked for a project manager who had a very strong personality. There was no arguing with him about anything. I learned quickly most things were easily left to his interpretation of right and wrong, and I did not have to provide my input unless requested to do so. Interestingly enough, he actually sought my opinions on food and sometimes on male/female communications and relationships. But even then, I realized many things we conversed on were subjective, so I always deferred to him for the conclusion.

During that project, I was assigned the task of writing a detailed white paper on the differences between one- and two-dimensional bar codes. You may know that bar codes are used in warehousing to track the location of goods. I did a lot of research and ended up buying a couple of text books on bar codes. I thought it was important I learn the basics first, since I knew very little of the subject before I began. One of the less interesting things I learned about bar codes is the correct spelling is two words: bar code, and not the common barcode or even bar-code as some spell checkers would recommend. This was a fact stated by a pretty reputable person in an authoritative book on the subject. So, throughout my paper, I used the correct spelling: bar code.

When I had completed a solid first draft of the paper, I handed it to my project manager for his review. He read through it and red-penned several parts. His only comment : You misspelled bar code; it should be barcode. I panicked because I knew he was dead wrong, but I knew correcting him would be a difficult task as well.

I had to do two things quickly: Persuade him the word was correct the way I wrote it and allow him to save face. I can honestly tell you this was a squeamish situation for me and my face began to turn hot and sweat began to leak out from all pores. To make matters worse, this was my first "confrontation" since I had gotten fired from my previous job as a software modeler. This exacerbated the situation because I was hoping to stay employed and get a strong positive review. I needed to be reassured that the last bad incident was not a dramatic personality flaw that would continue to rear its ugly head every time I had a conflict with a manager.

I took a deeeeeeeep breath and explained that the guy who literally wrote the book on bar codes uses the two-word spelling. I showed him the book to back up my claim. He stared at me for what seemed like way too long, but eventually he smiled and nodded his head and said, "Okay, I will leave it up to you to decide." His command to me was neither an admission of right or wrong. In this way he saved face, because I got to make the decision without having him admit he was wrong. That was it. I did it! It was definitely a bit clumsy but no bad feelings were formed as was evidenced by a remarkably strong review I received from this manager. (He actually claimed one of my strongest qualities was my ability to work well with others!) I was so relieved, the burning question I carried was now answered: No, I didn't possess any fatal character flaw that was going to doom me from being successful. Whew!

Almost a decade later, I was faced with a similar situation but I was able to maneuver much differently and with much more dramatic results. I was managing a project and my manager invited me to discuss our progress with his boss and his boss' boss. We launched into some of the issues we were having on the project and right before my very eyes and ears, my manager began to fabricate major misrepresentations. I was totally stunned. I wondered if he had more information than I did. I quietly began to write down the misrepresentations. I did not correct him. I did not challenge him. I smiled and demonstrated my support. One thing I did not do, however, was to collaborate on what I believed to be a misrepresentation. Remember, you must maintain your integrity above everything else, because if you lose that, you may never get it back.

After the meeting, my manager and I debriefed on what went well and next steps. I explained I had some discrepancies with some of the points he made, but I did not feel it was appropriate to deal with it in the meeting. He was pleased and thanked me for showing discretion. I allowed him to save face. Now that we were one-on-one, I still had to give him the opportunity to save face, again. I prefaced my questions with a sincere desire to understand: "I wasn't sure if things had changed since we last spoke, but I remember we agreed Paul would not be a good fit for the lead role on the sub-project. In the meeting, you stated Paul was being considered for this lead role, so does that mean there is new information?" To which he responded something like, "Oh, I'm sorry I forgot, you're right." And I continued, wanting to demonstrate I was truly trying to understand and I did support him, "I don't have a problem with Paul if he *is* your choice. We would just have some limitations we would have to work around, so I can go either way on that issue." He said he still thought Paul was a bad choice and he would personally tell the managers why Paul would not be considered for the sub-project lead role. As it turned out, my manager was legitimately nervous during the previous meeting and had literally forgotten the facts as we discussed. It made the situation much more real to me that even bosses can get scared in big meetings and forget what to say!

The Art of Making a Correction

A good rule of thumb is to ask yourself what is gained by making the correction? In a public situation, it is usually just a good stroking for your ego and also a bit of a power trip because you know more than someone else. I highly recommend you always save corrections for private. It almost never pays to correct someone in public, especially if it is someone who is a superior.

Next, ask yourself how important it is to make this correction. Is it petty? Every time you give someone feedback you run the risk of being misinterpreted. Therefore, think about the value of what you are doing. Is there meaningful value in providing the feedback? Is this just another opportunity for you to stroke your ego and show you are more knowledgeable? Be careful. Don't waste your manager's time unless you can add value.

Now, if you do have to move forward with the correction in private, check your attitude at the door. Any hint of arrogance will destroy the message you are to deliver. You should be clear in focusing on the facts or the acts. Be patient and give the person the benefit of the doubt. As Stephen Covey says, "Seek first to understand, and then to be understood."[4]

When giving feedback, always communicate clearly and speak in terms of what was said or done. Do not correct your manager directly as in, "You were wrong when you stated we had twelve hundred dollars in scrap material." Speak to what was said and in the context of trying to understand it. "The scrap was valued at twelve thousand dollars in the meeting. My numbers vary from that by more than 200 percent. I was hoping to better understand your assumptions so I might determine where I might be off in my calculations, since this will impact the total writeoff."

If appropriate, recommend a course of action. It's not enough to give feedback that something is out of place. If you are wrong and the information is correct, you may need to adjust your strategy. Having a recommended course of action shows your manager you're not part of the problem—by the very fact you have identified the problem you now are linked to it. By recommending a strategy to deal with the problem, you are now part of your manager's team to reach the desired objective.

Follow these guidelines and you can use opportunities like these to *strengthen* your relationship. My manager came to trust me so much, he asked for feedback on a regular basis. This was unusual for him, as I know he did not have such a relationship with anyone else. I attribute it to the trust and respect that developed in our relationship. I wanted to support him so he could be successful and he believed that *was* my motivation. This paid off, I was rewarded with increased visibility for my accomplishments, increased managerial responsibilities, the opportunity to network with high-ranking people in our company, and exceptional reviews, which translated to *money!*

A footnote to this chapter but one worth noting is on the art of surprise. Make it a practice *never* to surprise. I should have never walked into that cookie packaging materials meeting with my knowledge of the million-dollar scrap material without my boss understanding it, as well as his boss and his boss' boss. This would have given them the opportunity to determine how they wanted to deal with this "problem" and share the information, especially if it turned out a mistake was made by my department. Remember, how they manage this situation will impact how they are perceived by other departments and higher ups in the organization. Also remember, *there is nothing more embarrassing to a superior than to appear as if he or she does not have control over and is out of touch with his or her own department.*

Strategies to Meet Your Original Objective

We said earlier that almost all behavior and actions in the work place are rooted in some type of objective we are trying to accomplish. Therefore, if we stop certain sabotaging behaviors, we need to know the correct behaviors to replace them so we can still be effective in meeting our original objective. In this instance, we want to understand what type of behavior we can utilize that will allow us to be effective and show we are interested *without* people feeling we are trying to tell them what to do.

What I have found to be much more effective with men and women in the work place is an understanding I am not their mother. That is to say, my focus is that I am not committed to the outcome of a desired behavior of someone else. These people are grown adults. The final decision, right or wrong, beneficial or inefficient, is ultimately theirs to make. Everyone has a right to do things differently than you would do them.

Second, your 100 percent committed support must always be at forefront of your interactions with your superior. Even if he or she has chosen a different path than the one you suggested, you still have to give your support. Make it real and sincere. Remember, your number one job is to make your boss successful. If he or she is successful, you will be successful.

Third, don't ever take credit or say, "I told you so." There is no credit to be taken. If you are committed to your boss' success, it shouldn't matter who gets the credit for the idea. This is just a petty power trip to stroke your ego and you will fast find yourself at the short end of that power stick. Remember, ideas aren't promoted and developed, people are. People tell me this all the time: "He stole my idea." This is impossible. Ideas are impotent. Anyone can come up with an idea. What is remarkable is someone who can persuade others that an idea is worth putting resources and time and money against. People who work to make an idea a reality are special. By learning how to build successful relationships in the work place, you too will be able to realize your ideas.

Fourth, remember that your point of view can only be given as a recommendation. I recommend it be stated that way. Avoid saying anything that begins with the following phrases:

- "I don't agree because..."
- "That's wrong because..."
- "That's a bad move because..."

I have even gone so far as to *ask permission* from the other person before giving a recommendation. This is actually most effective in terms of being heard and retaining high credibility. The most prestigious position to be in is one where you are *requested* to give your opinion. Use caution, especially if your point of view differs vastly from the superior's point of view. Preface your ideas with a reminder that this is only your point of view. This will reinforce that you respect the other person's point of view and are humbled by the opportunity to add your own.

The only position to ever come from is one of sincere concern to help the other person. In the mother example, the tone is *condescending*. If your position is one of sincere concern to assist the other person in a decision, lose the attitude. No matter how much more knowledge or experience you have you will lose all credibility if you maintain a higher-than-thou attitude (another one of the qualities my manager ascribed to me on a review early in my career).

Most importantly, after you give your recommendation, let go of the outcome. This is something Mom never learned. She kept needling us over and over until we *finally* gave her the desired behavior. Do *not* make this mistake. Your role after giving any type of advice is to back off and allow the manager to make the decision. Especially where the manager has gone a different route than the one you suggested, you should verbally and physically show your 100-percent committed support.

The bottom line is to always ask permission to give an opinion, state it as a recommendation and remind the listener it is only your point of view, get out of the way and let the manager determine the course of action, verbally demonstrate your 100-percent support for the course of action, and *never* take credit for the outcome. Your reward will be a strong relationship with a manager who is *in your corner*. You have reinforced you are committed to his or her team and as your manager's success grows, so will yours.

CHAPTER THREE

Don't Show Loyalty Only to Yourself!

~━━◦◦◦◦◦◦━━~

*To be successful, the first
thing to do is fall in love
with your work.*

Sister Mary Lauretta, Roman Catholic nun

~━━◦◦◦◦◦◦━━~

Ah, the art of loyalty. This is probably one of the most fascinating aspects of business culture I have come to understand. The impact of this one can have huge implications to your career, either positive or extremely negative.

In November 1995, Buck Showalter was hired as the manager for a new major-league baseball team, the Arizona Diamondbacks. Prior to his hiring, no team existed. Therefore, Showalter had a unique opportunity to create a team that embodied *his idea* of what essentialized a winning team. When interviewed about how he was going to build the team, he replied, "I've managed a million games in my mind," he said. "It's not about managing games. It's about managing people and surrounding yourself with people you can trust and who have the same dream as you have, the same vision."[5]

The quintessential elements of loyalty, therefore, are trust and commitment to the same vision. It is not skill. A skill or years of experience or knowledge is something else other than loyalty. And what Buck Showalter was explaining was that the critical elements in selecting individuals for *his* team are trust and shared vision. Skill may make the top five list of desirable qualities, but it is not the first element. The results for Showalter and the Arizona Diamondbacks have been fantastic. The first year in the major leagues, the Diamondbacks boasted the fourth winningest record for an expansion team. The second year they won the pennant for their division.

Think of your current responsibilities in your job. If you had to take an inventory of the top three objectives in your current role, what would those objectives look like? Every time I ask this question in my workshops I get a multitude of answers—but rarely the correct one.

The number one responsibility for you in any role you will undertake is to make your boss successful. Period. If that is not at the top of your list, you are only being loyal to yourself. In other words, you are probably sabotaging your success and exhibiting trust destroying behavior because your focus is only on your own objectives. If you are going to demonstrate loyalty, you have to change your focus.

This is not to say you shouldn't have any responsibilities in your job. Rather, it means you should understand what your boss' vision is so you can prioritize your workload and responsibilities appropriately.

One important point of clarification is worth discussing and that is to what you direct your loyalty. In the "olden days" there was talk of company loyalty where employees pledged their entire careers to a single company. The companies rewarded those employees with security, a gold watch, and a pension.

In our culture today, there is no more company loyalty. Companies are entities that make business decisions to keep themselves competitive and profitable. People can be utilized or eliminated to meet that objective. So, how could there possibly be a place for loyalty in today's business climate?

The type of loyalty I have described is loyalty to a person. The relationships you develop with people are the investments you make in your career. As those people go places, get promoted, move on to other companies, they will take you with them. You will be picked to be on their teams. Successful leaders, like Buck Showalter, want to surround themselves with loyal and committed people. Therefore, a career is built on relationships and loyalty is the building block of those relationships.

Think of it this way: If you were promoted to a high level in your company and you had to pick your team, who would you pick? Would you pick people who were really smart and could get the job done but were cocky and out for themselves? Or would you pick people you knew you could trust to implement your vision, even though they might not be as smart as the other people I described. The bottom line is you want to surround yourself with people you can trust, people who are loyal and committed to you.

In Chapter Two I told you about when I was an inventory planner and took on additional work to make the team successful. I did not bother to check in with my boss on what his vision of the program was and so I developed my own vision and allowed all my energies and actions to support *my* vision.

The result? I was probably viewed as disloyal. When I put in a request to move to another department, my manager jumped at the opportunity to send me on my way. At the time, it didn't make sense that I could run a program successfully and not be valued by my management. But in retrospect, I defined what was success for the program. And although I did reach my objectives, I can't be sure I met my manager's objectives.

There is one point of complexity here I should explain as it is likely to be relevant to many of you. When I originally began the project, I sat down with management and defined the program objectives. Therefore, when I managed to objectives, there was management alignment.

During the course of the project there was a change in the organization and I got a new boss from an entirely different department, with a different view of operations. I never bothered to sit down with my new manager and try to understand his vision and what he saw as success for the program.

The bottom line is that I hadn't remained flexible to the change in visions. I assumed no changes. In addition, I didn't invest a lot in relationships, so I wouldn't have known if my original management's objectives had changed because I kept out of their hair. In my book of what made a good employee, it was as follows: Get the goal, run toward the finish line, and don't stop until you cross it. I guess I was a bit of a pit bull after all.

What Is Loyalty?

Loyalty is a shared vision. First, you need to understand what your boss' vision is. If you don't know, ask. If you are interviewing, this is a great question to ask. The vision will give you insight into how your boss views the world, what's important, what's extremely important, and what success is. From an interviewing perspective, you will have the basis to direct all your answers. From an employee point of view, you will have the basis on which to prioritize your work and energies.

Let's revisit the aftermath of the parting of ways between Jimmy Johnson, the former coach of the Dallas Cowboys, and

Jerry Jones, the owner. As I said back in Chapter One, when Coach Johnson started, the Cowboys' record was nothing to write home about. Eventually, Coach Johnson got the Cowboys to the Super Bowl and won—two years in a row!

So what happened? It appears from many articles published on the topic that Coach Johnson wanted control. Even though both Coach Johnson and owner Jones had the same vision—make the Cowboys number one—there was still a major difference of expectations as to how that would happen.

Coach Johnson clearly valued his independence and his way of doing things more than he believed or could commit to owner Jones. Coach Johnson insisted on doing things not in line with what owner Jones expected. When owner Jones looked back on that incident, he said, "In retrospect, it was those things that started me thinking about a change. My reaction to that, my lack of enthusiasm about [patching things up] told me where our relationship was headed."[6]

Already convinced Coach Johnson was no longer his man, owner Jones had one more encounter that pushed the situation to the limit, forcing Coach Johnson to leave. There is a story Coach Johnson related at a dinner party about owner Jones' need to appear to be in control. Coach Johnson claimed that before a draft pick announcement at a press conference in which ESPN was present, owner Jones stated to Coach Johnson, "You know the ESPN camera is in the draft room today. So whenever we're about to make a pick, you look at me, like we're talking about it."[7] Get it? Owner Jones wanted to appear in control. This forced Coach Johnson into a subordinate role since it would appear Jones had the final say.

According to many published accounts, Coach Johnson was retelling *this* story to some friends at an NFL dinner party, when he was approached by owner Jones, who wanted to make a toast. The other members at the table were friends of Coach Johnson, but had been fired by owner Jones in the past. As you might have guessed, they reacted rather coldly to owner Jones and he wasn't invited to stay. This apparent snub was the last nail in Coach Johnson's coffin, so to speak. Coach Johnson was clearly independent and overtly demonstrating loyalties elsewhere and finally humiliating owner Jones publicly.

Angrily, owner Jones addressed some reporters after the dinner and announced , "Five hundred coaches could have won the Super Bowl with our team." *Sports Illustrated*'s Jack McCallum interpreted Jones' tirade as "I'm the boss, he's just the coach. I'll fire him if I want to. He works for me."[8]

After a couple of weeks of attempted reconciliation, owner Jones and Coach Johnson agreed to part. Coach Johnson had the remaining five years of his contract voided and Jones offered Coach Johnson a two-million-dollar bonus. "I want to thank you for everything you've done for the Cowboys," Jones told Coach Johnson. "How does two million dollars sound?"

"Jerry, you don't have to do that," replied Coach Johnson

"Hey, I want to do it, you deserve it."[9]

Okay, so what's the bottom line here? Most of us screw up and don't get such rewards when asked to leave. The main point is Coach Johnson could not support owner Jones' vision. He didn't even respect the guy, as was evidenced by his public remarks. Jones wanted to feel in control and Coach Johnson ultimately could not follow. Coach Johnson ended up doing stuff to get himself mentally kicked off the team, until things got so bad Coach Johnson was asked to leave (he still had five years remaining on his contract). The fact that Jones *allowed* Coach Johnson to leave and *determined* Coach Johnson should get a bonus is consistent with his previous need to control the situation. The fact that he gave Coach

Johnson two million dollars shows Jones probably did appreciate Coach Johnson. Hard to comprehend but it was nothing personal and Coach Johnson left not so bitterly. At a press conference announcing the split, Coach Johnson said, "I can sincerely tell you that I feel better today about Jerry Jones as a friend than I have in our entire relationship."[10]

Good move on Jones' part, as Coach Johnson became a highly paid sports commentator for a major television network. Therefore, the last move Jones made would ensure Coach Johnson would be in his corner, perhaps, in future business dealings.

A personal example demonstrates the highly powerful nature of loyalty. I was working with a high-tech company to help them improve their business processes and install an enterprise resource planning system (ERP) software solution. During that time, I became involved with many of the key personnel who would have strong influence over whether the changes we were developing would stick and become part of the new culture.

In particular, there was a manufacturing site managed by someone who most (except senior-level management) agreed was not very effective. A nice guy, but not the kind of leader you would expect in such a responsible position. Some of his actions were actually slowing down if not impeding the business improvement development process.

I remember asking my boss, "Help me understand how someone like Bob gets hired into an incredibly well-paying job, performs mediocre at best, and is so highly regarded by management?" To which my incredibly insightful manager replied, "He's Dan's man." Dan was the vice president of operations, to whom Bob reported. Apparently, when he was being hired, Bob said to the CEO, "My job is to make Dan successful." And boom, he was hired and received great opportunities, in spite of being viewed by many as a mediocre performer.

Loyalty is a powerful concept, and I have tested it out many times only to get strong positive results. This brings us to the second point of what loyalty is: verbal support and acknowledgment of your boss' vision. If you know what your boss' vision is, show your loyalty by actually speaking the words, "I support your vision."

I was working for a very difficult manager on a very difficult project. He did not communicate regularly with anyone and I was finding it frustrating and completely disempowering not to know what was going on. I plowed through until I couldn't take it anymore and I sat down with him. Our conversation went something like this.

"I feel very upset and frustrated. My job is to make you successful and I don't feel I get enough support from you to make that happen."

He was completely shocked. He replied, "Your job is to make yourself successful."

I quickly reiterated, "It is to make you successful. I know if you are successful, this project will be successful, and ultimately, I will be successful. My focus begins with you."
He paused a minute, then responded, "What can I do to help you be more successful?"

After that respectful confrontation, he "adopted" me as his right-hand "man." I was on the inside track of just about everything. I had unbelievable opportunities to meet with his boss and his boss' boss. I was invited to co-deliver a presentation at the CEO level for a multi-billion-dollar company, which was uncommon for my level and experience.

Here's the real proof. Months after I rolled off that project and was no longer working for that manager, he was still trying to find opportunities for me to work for him. I had never experienced this type of response from a manager before. In addition, when I discovered an opportunity in his area, I immediately called him and said I'd love to help out on the project in any capacity. He usually couldn't wait for me to start.

In this situation I was doing the same type of high-quality work I had always done throughout my career. I worked well with my peers and was very resourceful. The only thing that had changed was my focus. Instead of focusing on the work, I focused on how I could make my manager successful. The work was important and quality was there but now it was in alignment with my boss' view of success.

This attitude played over into my relationship with him. If I saw an opportunity for him to be successful, I would quickly point that out and offer my assistance—in a recommendation format, of course. And likewise, if I saw danger ahead, I would point that out with a recommendation on resolving the matter. He began to trust me and as he began to see I was committed to his success, he became committed to mine.

He gave me high marks in front of the right people. I found I was able to have influence on the outcome of many key decisions. That's not to say that everything I ever recommended was moved to action. But a considerable amount of my recommendations were put into action—with favorable results for my manager. The positive cycle of commitment and loyalty continued.

The most important lesson I learned was how to sincerely maintain this focus on my manager's success. It meant recognizing he was the coach, so he made the final call and that was it. It also meant recognizing I was becoming the star player on the team—the quarterback—and it was within my responsibility to feed back what I saw as the winning plays. Did you know the quarterback can go out to the field with the team and change the plays? Well, I found I was able to do that as well. Even after we agreed on a course of action, I had built up enough trust that I could choose a modified course of action and find later I had his support, even when things did not turn out favorably.

What I discovered was he didn't want to call every shot, and so consequently, he appreciated I was able to step up to the plate and take the initiative and responsibility. However, unlike my past experiences, I earned the trust necessary to act somewhat independently and still maintain his strong support.

This brings us to the third point of what loyalty is. Loyalty is being committed to the success of your boss. You got the vision part down, you verbalized your support, and finally the driver of all your actions is ultimately your unwavering commitment to making your boss successful. The bottom line is if your boss is successful, he will receive opportunities to advance his career. As he moves in his career, he will want to build a loyal team around him, and you will be at the top of his list.

Recently SAP, one of the world's largest software makers of enterprise systems, lost its president of U.S. operations. He defected to Siebel, another software company—much smaller but experiencing rapid growth. What was so interesting about this move is he became the president of Siebel. And who do you think he picked to be on his team? A handful of vice presidents who worked with him at SAP.

Can Loyalty Be Misplaced?

Alex is one of the most successful salesman in his company. He is not what you would expect in a salesman. He is honest, sensitive, and introverted. What has been the secret of his success? His unwavering loyalty to his customers.

In his field, there are end customers and distributors, or middlemen. He discovered if he built strong alliances with the middlemen, he could concentrate a larger amount of business with fewer customers and provide better customer service for his territory.

The temptation other salesmen have faced is to sell to both the distributor *and* the end customer. The problem with that is if he sells to the end customer, he becomes a competitor with the distributor, who is *also* trying to sell to the end customer. While this seems to be a very straightforward concept, and Alex has earned the highest sales in the company to demonstrate the validity of his approach, there are still those in his company who cannot agree with his strategy. They simply believe more customers equals more sales.

For many years Alex worked for a manager who was able to support Alex's way of doing business. Alex was awarded plaques for salesman of the year and received a promotion into management. He trained his employees in his philosophies and the result was a very strong and prosperous territory.

In recent years, there have been management changes, namely the president. And now it appears the manager Alex reported to will be retiring soon. The new president is slowly building his team. He does not appreciate Alex's approach to business and customers. Alex is not going to change and feels strongly about his vision of success. This is causing a tremendous amount of stress for Alex.

Loyalty is a strange thing. It is important but must be properly placed. In this instance, Alex has built a successful sales territory by showing unprecedented loyalty to certain types of customers. The results have been phenomenal. However, the new president does not support that type of strategy. He wants to sell to everyone. The result is the new president is slowly pushing Alex out his job and into another role that won't produce a conflict.

This is frustrating to watch but sometimes we get so caught up in how we are performing we lose sight of the big picture. In the business culture, loyalty is an essential ingredient for longevity. Performance alone is not. Remember the example of Jimmy Johnson and the Dallas Cowboys? He clearly took that team from the bottom to the top in a few years but it did not help him retain his job in the end.

Clearly when management changes, loyalty must be re-assessed in terms of "what are this management's philosophies about people, customers, work, ethics, etc." If the new phi-losophies are diametrically opposed to your own and you cannot imagine changing your position, it is time for you to leave. If you do not take the initiative to leave on good terms, you will eventually be asked to leave on their terms.

Differing visions (between you and your boss) is never something that's discussed in career counseling as a red flag to change jobs. In my experience this is one of the most criti-cal opportunities to recognize as a legitimate time to take control and proactively look for something better suited for yourself. Control is an important element to have in your career and part of what I'm trying to impart to you is the knowledge for you to have more control. We will discuss this concept in more detail in the section, "But What If I Don't Agree With My Manager's Vision?"

Here's a great example of a woman I know who cleverly leveraged management change. She was the director of manu-facturing for a high-tech company and had worked for two different managers in less than six months. The first one had hired her into the company and she had a very good relation-ship with him. He was reorganized within the company and she found herself reporting to someone with whom she had previously been peers. There were many challenges working for this new manager—the main challenge being his paranoia and need to control everything. In any event, she and he did spend some time talking about potential next positions for her, although nothing materialized.

That manager was reorganized and a brand new manager was hired. She immediately sought this new manager out. She told him she was so happy he was onboard. Believe it, she was sincere, since anyone over the last manager was a radical improvement for her. Several weeks after he had started, she began to talk to him about some opportunities for career development that were kicked around with her former boss. After the discussion she confirmed she was happy where she was and had no plans to leave. She really nailed down her commitment.

Within a few months, her new manager made her an offer to take on a new, highly visible, and very exciting role in new product development. She almost fell off her chair she was so happy.

Let's take a quick recap of what she did. The new management is always a fifty-fifty risk in terms of making it work for you. There's a 50 percent chance it could work in your favor and a 50 percent chance it could work against you, especially if the new management already has expectations to hire someone other than you for your role. She built her new manager's confidence, assuring him she was glad he was there and she was committed in the long term. He responded in kind with development opportunities as part of *his* team. And that's exactly what new management does: build its own team.

Can You Be Too Loyal?

Let me tell you about taking loyalty to the extreme and having it backfire. Later on in my career I had begun to understand the importance of loyalty as, "I will do whatever you think I should do to make you successful." This is not quite right, as I'm sure you now understand. After too much wine at the annual company event, I wandered up to my senior manager and started with some pleasantries. I could tell he was a little uncomfortable; not realizing he was a little introverted, I began to wax on about how much I liked working on the last project with him. Then, as if someone hit the wrong button in my brain, I just started going on and on about how if he determines what the next "hot" skills are and seems to lack those in his organization, "I am the man. I will take whatever classes, courses, training…to get those skills. Just say the word."

I remember a horrified expression on his face, but he was polite and excused himself rather quickly. I felt awful, confused, and a little drunk. My intentions were to show my loyalty, but I knew it backfired. My suspicions were confirmed less than a month later when I was promptly reorganized out of my manager's department and reassigned to another. I felt terrible.

My first big mistake was I had too much to drink at a company event. If this ever occurs (by accident, of course), I recommend you refrain from opening your mouth and sharing opinions with anyone important.

Second, loyalty means showing support for another. It does not mean giving away *your* responsibility for your own actions and career to someone else. They may influence you, of course, but that goes without saying. In the end, you are responsible for your development. Period. If anyone tries to convince you otherwise, politely smile but do not be fooled. If you give this responsibility away, you have no one to blame but yourself if you end up going nowhere.

Third, over-exuberance may be a bit overwhelming for some, as it was for my manager, but it is definitely not going to create bad will. It's one of those things you really can't do too much of. It's like giving a compliment too much. As long as it's sincere, no one should ever be angry with you. I had many positive experiences with that manager later on in my career. He was very kind in strongly supporting a personal evaluation for me. I decided if I have to make a mistake, this was the least harmful type to make.

But What If I Don't Agree With My Manager's Vision?

A manager, Bill, I used to work for recently had drinks with me. He had enjoyed a very solid reputation at the company we had worked at, and was respected within the department as well as by other departments. Consequently, Bill had a lot of influence with highly visible projects and initiatives. There had been a reorganization and Bill had gotten a new director and boss. I found out one of the reasons Bill left the company was because when he was working for the new director it became very apparent the director did not want any feedback from him. During team meetings in which all the director's top ranking men were present, several, including my manager, presented different ideas than the director's and were quickly cut down. This became so frustrating for my manager, as well as the others, that Bill eventually understood the director did *not want* participation in the business decision. In other words, he wanted trusted managers, and people to *execute* his plan. My manager realized he could not support the director's vision and he did not want to work in an environment where he had little influence. So he happily left.

I love this story because of the simplicity of it. Number one, my manager was already successful and highly respected. Number two, after the reorganization, he began to ascertain he could not support his new boss' vision. Number three, he realized he had to leave.

How many of us were ever taught or encouraged to consider changing jobs when our vision and our boss' vision are out of alignment? Well, if any of you raised your hand, good job. As for me, I never even conceived of this as an option. I thought if things weren't working with my boss, I should just try harder. But I wouldn't consider leaving. You leave to take a development step or more money or more quality time at home. The idea of vision alignment was completely unheard of.

One of the steps we missed as we've talked through this chapter is your own inventory of your vision, principles, and ethics. You need to know what is important to you and on what you could never compromise. This list varies by individual and also the degree as to which you could compromise.

In other words, there aren't black and white or right and wrong guiding principles. There are degrees of how comfortable you could be in compromising. Therefore, it is important to know where you stand on these issues.

One of the exercises I've used to define my guiding principles is to identify experiences I've had in the past that left me feeling ashamed of my behavior and with regret. I've tried to look across the three main areas of my life: myself, my work, and my personal relationships.

In my work, I've been ashamed when I've acted without integrity and sacrificed everything for reaching the objective. Therefore, I'm now able to identify integrity as a guiding principle I want to demonstrate throughout my career. And I know when things get difficult, that's when I will build and strengthen my character by demonstrating this principle. I've defined integrity as being open, caring, honest and truly concerned with the betterment of others. I want to earn the right to be trusted by others.

Next, consider the vision and style of your manager. Are they aligned with your own? As I said, it's not a perfect fit but rather a degree of match you can live with and feel good about. Is there a fit? If there isn't, now you are in a position of power to control the next steps you take in your career. Rather than stay in the job and suffer, you can identify there is a bad fit and begin to build your strategy for the next step you want to take in your career.

My friend went to marriage counseling because her husband changed a lot after they got married. He used to be fit, but since their marriage he had gained twenty or thirty pounds, stopped exercising, and resumed smoking, a habit my friend detested. In addition, he had become a complete slob and left clothes everywhere except in the laundry basket. This lifestyle was vastly different than what she had originally expected: healthy person who was somewhat organized.

She went into marriage counseling with a list of all her husband's flaws. During the session, she began complaining about how he never exercised. She fully expected the counselor to raise her eyebrows and exclaim, "What? He *never* exercises?! What is the matter with him? Let's put together a strategy he can live with that will help him exercise."

Instead, the counselor looked over at my friend's husband and sympathetically said, "That's okay, most Americans don't exercise."

The bottom line is that my friend had to accept her husband, warts and all, or get out of the marriage. She never guessed that would be the solution. The counselor explained, "You have a choice. You can accept him like he is or don't accept him and end the marriage. The fact that he's changed is not relevant." The fact he does not meet her expectations is not relevant. What is relevant is whether she can accept him as-is.

This is the same assumption we must make in our relationships with our boss. Under most circumstances, the vision of our leaders is pretty solid. That's a starting point for any leader—to have a vision. That's why it makes sense to learn the vision early on in your relationship. Once you realize you can't support the vision, you are in the best position to accept the situation and empower yourself to change your situation. By doing this, you now have the control to maintain a good relationship with your boss. There is always some value to remaining on good terms for future reference. In other words, it's a small world and you never know when this person may be able to still exert some influence on your life.

Remember the story I told you earlier about my getting fired? Well, there is a postscript to that story. A couple of years ago, I was consulting on one of the largest projects on the West Coast and guess who I ran into? The manager who fired me showed up at a project meeting and I almost fainted. He was working for another company.

Right after he fired me, I had the sense to look him in the eyes and shake his hand and say, "I really wish you the best. It's too bad it didn't work out." At least I had made a clean exit. Now, almost three years later, he came up and shook my hand and said, "How are you doing? Good to see you!" There is power in keeping the relationship on positive terms so you can take career steps and have the support to do so.

The final point of loyalty is that it is based on perception. That is, your loyalty can only be perceived. It is somewhat subjective. Therefore, it takes time to build loyalty, just as it takes time to build a relationship. Your loyalty and trust will be tested every time you have the opportunity to interact with your manager. Sometimes you will make mistakes. The power of a good relationship is that in making mistakes you would not be perceived as disloyal.

I've asked my workshop participants what they think the time period is in building strong loyal relationships. The answers vary, and based on my experience it varies. If you are awkward and learning this stuff for the first time, figure about a year to solidify your loyalty. If you are more adept at this, it could happen with significant regular interaction in a few months. The bottom line: Be patient. It's an ongoing process.

Loyalty Isn't Even Skin Deep

As you've probably discovered, loyalty is one of the central dynamics to establishing trust in a relationship. One of the bits of research I came across as I was writing this book was a survey that was done on 211 college campus career center professionals. This is interesting because these are the people who are providing career coaching to us as we leave college and graduate school. Remember what I said earlier in the book about how much of what you learned in school is wrong in developing success in the work place? Here's more evidence that the school system doesn't get it.

The survey had the career center professionals rank eleven attributes in order of the priority they *think* employers look for in a candidate. The result? Loyalty was listed at ten, which was below the attribute of beauty. That is, career center professionals thought it was more important to be attractive than loyal. What came in last? The ability to start immediately. Okay, so now we know at least we didn't miss this in school. They never even taught it—because they didn't get it.

Many Women Don't Get It

In the 1980s a survey was undertaken by Edith and Arthur Highman to discover what it takes for a woman to be successful in business. The survey was conducted over several companies and consisted of about a thousand respondents. The participants were both male and female and were at the director level and higher.

One of the most enlightening questions the Highmans asked was simply, "What does it take for a woman to be successful in business today?" When they asked women, the number one response was to get the results. When they asked men, they ranked the women's number one answer third! The number one answer given by the men was the women's ability to develop relationships and fit in. These men made up the majority of the top slots in corporations across America.

Based on what I've read, I conclude many of those successful women in the Highman's study had probably secured strong relationships but didn't realize it had been a critical component of their success. Early on when I began researching this topic, I focused on the women's perspective. Many of the published books on successful women fail to make a connection between strong superior and subordinate relationships and success. Many of the books I've read on the subject seem to suggest how important it is for women to control how others (men) perceive them. Power and how to use it becomes the main issue. We will spend significant time in later chapters discussing power and its role in the work place relationship.

Building Loyalty in a Relationship Is Like Small Tests

Loyalty builds over a period of time. Each interaction you have with your superior can become another opportunity to test and prove your loyalty.

My friend, Alan, employed a worker, Stuart, from almost the inception of his business. Alan knew about business but he knew nothing about running an office. But Stuart did. Stuart helped Alan hire a staff, he took care of administrative things from getting personalized stationery to providing financial analysis of the business. Stuart also alerted Alan when he believed Alan's partner was stealing from him. Some years, especially in the beginning, were lean years and Alan's business survival was questionable. However, Stuart stayed, worked hard, and rarely complained.

About four years later, I met Alan and eventually I worked on his company's books. It did not take long for me to discover that good old Stuart had been embezzling thousands of dollars from Alan's business. Two weeks after I took over the books, Stuart gave his resignation, as I had predicted. Amazingly enough, Alan was not furious at Stuart for stealing from him. He explained, "He took what he took but he was still loyal all those years. I should have seen it coming. Stuart had developed a gambling problem and that probably drove him to do this. But the bottom line is, I would still help him if he needed my help."

And I can tell you that was the case. Alan has had the opportunity to work with Stuart (as an independent contractor) and has happily assumed the relationship. When Alan required a short-term loan, Stuart actually came through with a quick loan at no cost. This reinforced Alan's belief that Stuart was genuinely loyal to Alan.

In another situation, Alan hired a worker named Sylvia to help him in the office. Sylvia was highly recommended to Alan by people whose opinions he greatly respected. He expected only good things from Sylvia. She was a terrible worker, as my own eyes observed. Other people in the office commented on her lack of work ethic to Alan but he did not really change his opinion of her too much.

As Alan was getting ready to leave on a one-week vacation, he gave Sylvia an assignment. When Alan returned, she complained she did not even have time to look at the assignment. In his eyes, this was her first failure in terms of "testing" her loyalty. A second test came when she was calculating final money due to her end of employment with Alan. Previously, it had been agreed she would be working for Alan temporarily for a full three-month period, after which he may have an opportunity for her to work on a permanent part-time basis. As the three-month period lapsed, she gave Alan final instructions regarding pay due to her. As it turned out, her calculations were incorrect, and her underlying assumptions were based on fabrications. As Alan learned of her deceit, he became less patient with her.

The third and final test of loyalty was how Sylvia handled the disagreement over the final calculations of her last payments. She blurted out Alan could not be trusted to keep his word and he went back on what he had initially promised. She proceeded to make threats to his ability to do business in the future and how she would ensure it would be difficult for him. That was it.

What was so interesting is that the dollar value of the argument was not even a thousand dollars and yet this act was considered much more heinous than what Stuart did, which netted in thousands of embezzled dollars. Simply put, while Alan viewed Stuart as loyal, he did not lose good feelings toward him; since he viewed Sylvia as very disloyal, he vowed never to do business with her in any capacity.

Rewards of Being Loyal

I promised you I would tell you what you have the right to expect in your relationship with your boss. This is the reward for your loyalty. If you are not generating these types of benefits, perhaps your boss is not being loyal to you.

Number one: the ability to work independently. Remember back in Chapter One when we listed the qualities our managers had perceived as negative in our behaviors? Independence is frequently listed as a negative characteristic. The bright side is that with a solid relationship, you can act more independently. The reason is that your manager believes you will be acting in his or her best interest.

Frequently what occurs when you don't have a solid relationship and/or you've already given reasons to support the fact you are not loyal is that your manager can become uncomfortable even neurotic about controlling you. An over-controlling boss can be a red flag that you have been behaving in a way that has destroyed trust. Since your boss doesn't believe you are out for his or her best interests, your boss becomes paranoid about your actions and clamps down control over you.

I frequently hear that managers have the undesirable management style of micro-managing. In my experience, I have seen this is not a style issue or even the problem. It's actually an indication that something is wrong in the superior/subordinate relationship. In other words, there is a lack of trust.

In the example I gave earlier in the book about my experience as an inventory planner, I never did check in with the new management to get their vision on how to run the project. As a result, my boss told me I was too independent. Since he didn't have reason to believe I was out to make him successful and support his vision, it made sense he wanted more input on my work. Had I established a solid relationship with him early on, he would have been confident I was executing his vision and I would have been able to work more independently. He would have probably seen my independence as positive.

The second benefit of being loyal is the ability to make decisions. As I said in the beginning, the art of business politics is not learning how to be agreeable and saying yes. That would kill most of our spirits. The real fun of working is being able to make decisions that have power and influence in the organization. Once again, the secured relationship with the boss allows this type of independent action. The bottom line is if your boss knows you are committed to his or her success, your boss is confident the decisions you make will be in his or her best interest.

The third benefit of being loyal is probably one of the most important aspects of the relationship. It is the ability to make mistakes. When you feel everything you do has to be perfect or else you'll wind up with a pink slip, that is probably another red flag you haven't built a trusting relationship with your superior. Making mistakes is part of being human. Therefore, since we know it will happen, we must plan for it. The best insurance you have is in building strong relationships. Your superior can protect you when you fall and give you the support to resume.

The fourth benefit of loyalty is protection, which involves your manager fighting for your reputation. Your manager has a direct interest in seeing you succeed and is committed to helping you shine. Everyone needs a sponsor to move up in any organization. This person has got to be willing to fight for you and stick with you, even when you're down. This is the ultimate test of loyalty.

The fifth benefit of loyalty is in being provided development opportunities and promotions. As you demonstrate your commitment to your boss's success, he or she should do the same in kind for you. Part of creating your success is in supporting your development. You will also be able to leverage your relationship in seeking out your own opportunities in the organization or even outside of the organization.

The sixth benefit of loyalty is flexibility. This is probably one of the most important benefits in our work place today. Having flexibility in work schedule or work office can greatly impact our quality of life.

After two years of traveling, I went to my management and asked if there was an opportunity for me to stay local for a year or so. I explained my husband and I had been trying to have a baby for almost two years with no luck. Part of the problem was I was traveling so much. The response? My manager asked, "What do we have to do to keep you here?" That was a key sign I had successfully built a trusting relationship. The payoff? I was allowed to transfer into another department for several months, which allowed me to eliminate almost all travel from my schedule.

Within five weeks of starting my new role, my husband and I adopted a beautiful baby boy. Anyone who has experienced adoption understands it can be a big surprise when you find out a baby is available. We essentially got a call when I was in the middle of a business trip. I had no idea we would be adopting so soon.

I read through my company's policy regarding adoption and learned I could defer my leave for up to four months. Originally, I had agreed to take the position for only five or six months, basically filling in for someone else who was on maternity leave. In addition, my company was beginning its annual assessment process, which was a very long and involved evaluation program. It involved compensation and promotional decisions for the entire consulting organization.

It became clear if I did decide to leave, which I could have legally done, I would be leaving a truckload of work behind me and the organization was not well equipped to fill my position for that period. I made a decision to defer my maternity leave for four months and stay in my new role and successfully support the annual assessment process. It was grueling. I was working up to sixteen hours a day. My nanny only worked fifty hours a week so my husband ended up filling in for the other thirty or so hours I worked late into the night.

My manager was so happy I sacrificed my leave to support the group, she allowed me to work out of my house for almost three months. That was unheard of in the department. Some people got to spend maybe a day or two telecommuting, but five days for three months was completely unconventional.

When I received my review after only four months on the job, I got an excellent rating. I was surprised because of the short duration of my role. But my boss recognized me as having "unquestionable loyalty and commitment." Having the flexibility to telecommute and have variable work hours greatly enhanced my personal situation.

Another story demonstrates how difficult it can be to get flexibility on the job without good relationships. My friend was working for a consulting company in New Jersey for almost a year before she left on maternity leave. She was a graphics person and worked significant overtime, even during her pregnancy. She had lots of friends in the department and overall loved her job. The only complaint was she couldn't stand her boss.

She felt her boss was always on a power trip trying to control her and getting her to conform with the department policies. Considering many of the policies wrong or unfair, she focused on her relationships with her peers and tried to ignore her boss.

My friend decided when she was out on maternity leave she would love to come back to the company and work only part-time. She had learned her boss had left the company and moved out West. Before her boss left, she had given my friend a performance review, which was also shared with the boss's boss. The review was not very good and emphasized a lot of the negative characteristics we saw back in Chapter One.

When my friend spoke to her boss's replacement about coming back to work part-time, the replacement sounded positive and said she would call her back. What do you think happened? Even though the boss was no longer there, there were other people in management who had come to develop a negative impression of my friend. The result? There was zero flexibility. They told her if she couldn't come back full-time with the expectation of working significant overtime, she should consider resigning. And that's exactly what she did.

How Loyalty Can Get You a Raise

One of the most uncomfortable situations arises for us once a year when we get reviewed and receive some kind of salary adjustment. While there are several types of negotiation styles that can be utilized to extract a little more money or title, one of the most effective means to that end is leveraging your loyalty.

A great story demonstrates how loyalty can be leveraged. My friend, Victor, had been at a company a little more than a year and had been very disappointed: the company was in the midst of downsizing, the revenue was down, there was a hiring freeze, and people were leaving because morale was so bad. Victor's annual evaluation approached. Even though the overall climate in the company seemed dismal, Victor's department had more influence and power and he thought he would be able to leverage this to his advantage. However, this still would require some preparation and well-spoken demands.

He organized his thoughts before the meeting for his review and also did some homework. He knew the technology he was helping to develop at this company was old compared to what was being used in other companies. His company was not investing in newer technologies, which was hurting Victor's personal career development. In addition, he found out his skill set was worth at least another seven to ten thousand dollars more if he decided to leave this company.

On the day of his review, Victor listened as his manager, Greg, recited all the great accomplishments he had made that year. Overall the evaluation rating was exceptional. Then Greg said he was sorry he could only get Victor an increase in salary of twelve hundred dollars because of budgetary constraints that were out of his control. He told Victor he felt badly and Victor deserved more.

Victor handled the situation like a pro. First Victor gave a pleasant smile and paused. He demonstrated he was humble and grateful for the evaluation rating. He expressed his gratitude and sincerely thanked Greg for the opportunity to have worked with other departments and was pleased to have discovered the other departments felt good about his work.

As he had Greg agreeing with him and feeling positive, Victor went through some of the lower ratings on the evaluation and asked Greg for ways he could bring those ratings to the highest level. Greg provided suggestions, Victor nodded and agreed he would make those improvements to his performance.

After both had agreed on Victor's strong performance, Victor switched gears and talked about Greg's vision for the department. Victor commended Greg on his vision and adamantly stated his full support of it. In addition, Victor stated he was committed to helping Greg fulfill his vision and Victor wanted to be one of the first to lay the groundwork. This clearly demonstrated Victor's overwhelming loyalty to Greg.

Victor began to talk of his commitment in terms of his personal situation. He described his commitment in staying with this company because it was in the location he wanted to be in. His family was close, he had a steady girlfriend, and he was in the middle of a master's program at the university. He was physically and mentally tied to staying put. He was not going anywhere. This built upon Victor's commitment by emphasizing his personal situation was complementary to his professional goals.

Victor recalled his past performance over the last year, but not in terms of accomplishments—he recalled his acts of *loyalty*. Specifically, he recalled the times he was patient and supportive with the department, even though Greg had made very specific promises related to what Victor should expect. None of those promises were kept, such as getting newer technology which would have allowed Victor to increase his marketability. Victor bided his time and hunkered down on the older and outdated technology, never complaining.

Victor posed a favor. "I have shown patience and willingly accommodated the direction of the department, and now I'm asking you for a favor." Victor showed his talk of loyalty was not just talk but he had solid evidence of a strong loyal track record over the last year. "While I can appreciate the severe financial pressures the company is experiencing, and I do appreciate the raise, it does not meet my expectations. I'm asking you for a favor, I need at least five thousand dollars to feel good about my position here." At this point, Victor had probably made the case for the increase, however, he realized this company was having trouble paying its own bills so it was not very likely he would be given the $5,000 in the next six months. Victor decided he had to create a sense of urgency without coming across as threatening.

Victor began to describe his personal situation, which was compelling him to require such an increase. He was putting himself through graduate school with no company reimbursements, and he was living on his own in Philadelphia and costs were going up. He finally pleaded his current salary just would not cut the bills and eventually something would have to give. He had brilliantly created a sense of urgency, without alienating himself in the process. He didn't have to bring up the fact his market value was seven to ten thousand dollars more and if his company didn't give him more money, he would find someone who would. And yet that was subtlety understood.

Another, more complex strategy here, was that Victor recognized he was not talking to the person who had the final authority to grant the additional money. That person was his boss's boss, the CFO. Victor had to acknowledge and coach his boss to go to the CFO and ask for more money and provide his boss with the persuasive justification that would win him the additional money.

In asking for the favor, Victor actually said, "I'm asking for a big favor here. I need you to go to Mike and ask for more money." Victor gave Greg the solid points he was able to use to convince the CFO. What were those points? His solid track record of loyalty and his personal and professional commitment to the company. Remember, his actual performance did not play much of a part at this point because that already got him the good review and twelve hundred dollars.

The result? Not only did Victor get the raise within a week, it was also retroactive for the last pay period! This was incredible, considering his manager later said, "Look, we are going to give you this raise, but please do not let anyone know about this as no one will be receiving raises this year, in the entire company!"

And one final point here. Within a very short time Victor's reporting relationship changed. He reported directly in to the CFO. Not only did he get the increase in money, but he built a relationship, a strong one based on demonstrated loyalty and commitment.

The moral of this story is that great work may only get your foot in the door. It's the price of entry. Your demonstration of loyalty, patience, and support of the vision of your superiors builds strong relationships and opens up the doors of opportunity!

In summary, here are the elements of successfully asking for a raise:

1. Confirm accomplishments on the evaluation.

2. Show gratitude and sincerity that the company values your work and express the enjoyment you have had working there.

3. Go through the portions of the evaluation that are not highest ranking and get feedback how to improve performance.

4. Listen to feedback and agree to take steps to improve performance.

5. Talk about the boss's vision for the company and how you are aligned with it, and your support and desire to be part of the energy to make it successful.

6. Thank your reviewer for the good review and the salary increase. Explain you were hoping for at least (fill in the blank). The word "hoping" shows you are flexible and willing to negotiate. Be ready to back up your claim on why you think you deserve more money. Keep a log of your accomplishments and overtime to justify your request.

7. Introduce your personal situation that further demonstrates commitment: to be close to family, where you live, dedicated to making this successful, and so forth.

8. Recall your loyal behavior over the last year; certain things you may have been promised that did not occur that you were patient with, did not complain about, and made every effort to make your boss successful.

9. Create a sense of urgency by discussing personal situation, such as you are putting your husband through school, have only one income, have two children, can't make it on current income.

I had a woman in one of my workshops, Chelsea, who successfully used this technique in a previous job. She was hired into a cruise line as a financial manager and was promised many developmental opportunities. After a year of back-breaking work, she received a good review and some money. She felt the company owed her more because it had not made good on its original promises.

Chelsea recalled how loyal and hardworking she had been throughout the year. She had not complained and did an excellent job to support the direction (vision) of her manager. She was hoping she could receive a little more at the end of the year as goodwill from the company that it wanted to keep her and valued her.

The result? Chelsea was promoted to director. She said it was the most wonderful seven years at a job she ever spent. She had healthy relationships, felt committed and loyal to her management, and was rewarded and valued by the company.

Don't Make This Mistake

My friend Barbara was hired into a new position by a new company and given a very high position reporting to the president of the company. She was making much more money than she had been making previously. She had been on the job nearly three months and had already demonstrated her worth. She cut costs and improved productivity by 30 percent! As she was helping to grow the business, she realized she needed additional support in her organization. Even though a hiring freeze existed throughout the company, she was so influential, she was able to hire a "number two" man under her who was making nearly the same salary she was.

At first she thought this is great. What influence she has had in the organization to bring in some great talent and be able to pay current market salary! But she began to feel badly because she clearly had more responsibility than this new guy and yet he was demanding almost the same salary as hers. She began to do some research and found out she was actually underpaid both within the company in her position and within her industry. She had only been with the company less than three months but had produced great measurable results and had started to feel justified in asking for more compensation.

Barbara told me of her dilemma. To make matters worse, her husband had been out of work for six months and they just had their second baby. Needless to say, she needed the extra cash. She told me she was going to go to her boss and demand a pay raise because she was underpaid and her husband was out of work. This was a big mistake, in my opinion.

My advice was simple: Wait until the formal scheduled six-month review. Loyalty takes a while to demonstrate. I recommended she wait until management presented her with a performance review and a proposed salary increase—and that she then negotiate. It is incredibly risky to ask for more money just because your situation changes and your family needs the money. If those are the driving factors, your odds of getting the raise are low. Management could view Barbara as not being a good team player. They could see her as concerned with herself and disloyal. This could be the beginning of some bad will between Barbara and her management. So don't make this mistake!

Here are the detailed points on how Barbara should proceed:

- Wait until her formal review before discussing any money.
- Do her homework and find out what her compensation should be.
- Know what her bottom line contributions are: increased revenue and decreased costs (these increase the wealth of the organization).

Barbara needs to continue to demonstrate exceptional capabilities and keep a personal log of these accomplishments in the event they could possibly go unnoticed or undocumented for the review. In Victor's case, he had mentioned additional accomplishments to his manager, such as the percent of overtime and weekend hours worked to meet the company's demands and project deadlines. These hours were not part of his company's review process since he was salaried and the recording of overtime was not necessary because Victor received no overtime compensation. But recording this information proved valuable in justifying Victor's commitment to the company during his review.

Barbara should continue to develop positive relationships with influential people, such as those people to whom she reports and people with whom she has contact and are part of the review process. She can take advantage of the next six months and continue to establish a "friendly" relationship with these people since their input can directly affect her career. Victor was always aware of the people he interacted with who were responsible for providing input for his review.

After he had completed a task or meeting with these people, he would personally follow up with them even though his manager did not ask him to.

For example, after completing an application for the litigation department, Victor contacted the paralegal responsible for the department and asked how things were going. Although there were no problems, Victor had made suggestions for an update process that provided more information for the user with status messages on the screen and an automatic report displaying updated accounts. The paralegal was very excited and said she would appreciate the work. Since Victor already knew the program, it took him very little time to complete this task. The paralegal's gratitude was shown as she personally went to Victor's manager and commended Victor for his efforts. If there were problems, Victor could help, and they saw he took a special pride in his job and the company.

Steps for achieving an increase at the formal review
Step One: Confirm accomplishments on the evaluation (performance).

This can be difficult for some who find it hard to listen. If Barbara doesn't listen to the entire review and make mental notes of how well she performed in respective areas, it could contradict the next step (Step Two) or require an explanation from her. Therefore, she should try not to interrupt during the review. Barbara should let the reviewer complete his "spiel" and say what he has been prepared to say. Unless the reviewer pauses for an expected response, Barbara should be nodding in agreement with a smile to acknowledge.

Step Two: Show gratitude and sincerity that the company values your work and express the enjoyment you have had working there (humility).

Most managers expect humility from their subordinates. Plus, this is an important strategy in negotiating. If you want to get someone to do something, rather than telling the person to do it and getting him or her on the defensive, you want to get the person on your side. If the person is on your side, this becomes evident when he or she is smiling and nodding in agreement with you. Since Barbara's boss already agrees with the results of her review, her agreement of those areas where there is no question of the abilities will get the reviewer on Barbara's side.

Step Three: Go through the portions of the evaluation that are not highest ranking and get feedback on how to improve performance (performance).

Step Three becomes easier to deal with after Step Two because the reviewer is providing positive feedback from a "happy" emotional state. Feedback is always important, as well as determination and willingness to improve in areas essential to success in the company.

Step Four: Listen to feedback and agree to take steps to improve performance (humility).

Step Four happens in conjunction with Step Three. These two are directly dependent on each other in a review. You can't have enough humility.

Step Five: Talk about the boss's vision for the company and how you are aligned to it (loyalty).

Step Five is good in that it reinforces loyalty, commitment, and interest. Too many people work just to collect a paycheck. Too few people show a lot of interest in their job or mention an interest in the future of their organization using quotes from their boss as a message of encouragement. The loyalty is demonstrated by agreeing to the future direction of the position and/or the company.

Step Six: Express gratitude for the review and salary increase and explain you were hoping for more. "I appreciate the increase and strong review, but I was hoping for at least (fill in the blank)."

If we assume after the reviewer has done his "spiel" (Step One) and mentioned the increase in pay, Barbara can start with the money issue. The reason being is these issues are independent of the areas on the review and the future of the organization. These are reasons for the money demands. The reviewer might feel like he is being "played" if personal situations are mentioned before a raise is requested. Nobody likes to feel like they are being taken.

Barbara could say something like, "Although my (percent or dollar amount) raise in pay is a considerable increase, I was hoping my income would increase (percent or dollar amount)." By saying "hoping," Barbara shows she had expected a higher raise, but she was aware she might not receive it. This is important in the negotiating process because Barbara has the ability to come to terms on an agreed amount. If Barbara were to simply use the word "expecting," it may seem she is dead set on a specified amount and negotiating might not be possible. Showing unwillingness to negotiate shows stubbornness and an inability to reason or rely on someone in difficult situations.

After the money statement, Barbara should wait for the infamous, "Why do you think you deserve that?" or "How do you justify that number?" Even if the reviewer says no to her requests, Barbara is in a position to begin with the supporting information to back up the deserved amount. Although it is unlikely the reviewer can give an immediate yes or no answer on the spot, Barbara should show him why she deserves this.

Of course, if the reviewer says "yes" immediately, Barbara should just say "thanks." In Victor's case, he was told the company wasn't in the position to give out raises at that time. However, he had guided his boss down the path where Victor expected him to say that and Victor began to justify his demand starting with "I understand the position of the company, however, I feel I am justified in this amount and here's why...." It was important Victor wait for his boss to complete his explanation of why the company could not meet his request and maintain eye contact with responsive, affirmative "head bobs" throughout his rebuttal. This showed the boss, once again, Victor understood and respected both his boss' and the company's position.

Victor worked with a guy, Paul, who never knew how to do that. He would make a statement that was completely unjustified. When someone rebutted him, he would look down at the paper in front of him and shake his head "no," showing his disagreement and inability to reason. The person rebutting Paul would raise his or her voice noticeably as Paul's head continued to move. Not only did this put the other person immediately on the defensive, but it also gave Paul a negative reputation of being a difficult person to work with. Even though Paul was older than Victor and started working at the company earlier, Victor was able to quickly receive additional responsibilities with higher level projects. Victor also made more money.

Step Seven: Recall loyal behavior over the last year—certain things that were promised that did not occur that you were patient with, did not complain about, and made every effort to make your boss successful (loyalty).

Step Seven is the next point to mention. Barbara's continued loyalty to the organization, as well as anything she was promised to receive (such as a promotion, added responsibilities, and so forth) which did not occur can directly influence the desired raise. Loyalty is demonstrated by past-year performance, overtime to get the job done, patience during any difficult periods, and a drive to make the organization successful. The point about making the boss successful can be perceived as though the boss does not have the ability to be successful on his own. Therefore, reflecting on production increases within Barbara's responsibility (the plant), as well as how her success contributed to that of the company, underscores her role as an important person loyal to her position and the organization. This also demonstrates her reliance on her boss as a superior.

Also, Barbara should stay away from the word "complain." Instead of the reviewer feeling grateful she didn't complain, he should feel grateful for the past year of tremendous successes that exceeded expectations.

Step Eight: Introduce a personal situation that further demonstrates commitment.

Backing up Step Seven on loyalty by describing how personal life is structured to support a long term company commitment is admirable. Many times employers are not aware of the sacrifices individuals are willing to make for the good of the organization.

Step Nine: Create a sense of urgency by discussing personal situation.

Step Nine provides reassurance that Barbara's demands will not fall by the wayside. Victor knew if he did not accent a level of urgency, his boss would probably have either never gotten back to him, or easily passed him off with a "Well, although we can't do it now, we'll try to do something comparable at your next review..." Victor didn't want to be pushed aside. Besides, he probably would have started interviewing at other companies if Victor had gotten a response like that.

Sometimes, people are afraid to mention their personal situation as a reason for needing a raise.

In Victor's case, he would have been satisfied if his company, instead of giving him a raise, would have offered to pay his MBA tuition. Barbara might want to mention the truth about her husband being unemployed. That way, her company could offer her husband a position, assuming he's qualified. Barbara, as well as her husband, would be happy if he did get the job offer.

This story has a happy ending. Barbara waited to make her demands for more money until the annual review. She got a terrific raise at the end of her first year. She continues to build strong relationships.

How Loyalty Can Make You An Awesome Manager

As you move along in your career, you understand the importance of building strong relationships above you in the organization. But what about below you? If you are going to succeed, you need to be thinking about who you would pick to be on your team. Whom can you trust to follow your vision and be committed to your success?

A student at one of my workshops who had been in consulting for about seven years had recently landed a vice-president position in a billion-plus-dollar company. He felt he had been picked for the position because of the strong relationships he had built with the senior management in the organization while he had been a consultant.

His concern was how to get his subordinates to do things. He admitted in the past his relationship with his subordinates was essentially a dictatorship. He would yell commands and basically control everything. He was beginning to realize that method of managing would not be effective in his new position. Even though he had learned how to build relationships up in the organization, he had failed to recognize the importance of building relationships down in the organization. Subordinates probably didn't trust him and assumed he was simply out for himself.

This is a costly mistake managers and companies make. The cost of losing a valuable employee chews up precious resources, time, and money. You have the cost of having to recruit and train just to get someone who can replace the lost employee. In addition, all the time that could have been invested in building a relationship is gone. Now a new relationship has to be developed.

Investing in the people you have now is the most cost-effective way of operating. Develop trusting relationships with them. Now that you have the insight of what builds and destroys relationships, you can coach them to become better subordinates. The payoff for you will be a pool of loyal and devoted people you can pick to be on your team. These people will work to make you successful.

You are now on your way to becoming a long-term success in your career. In addition, you will have the pleasure of helping others achieve their own success and happiness as well.

CHAPTER FOUR

Don't Avoid Opportunities to Schmooze!

And the trouble is, if you don't risk anything, you risk even more.

Erica Jong (1942–), American writer

Courage is the price that Life extracts for granting peace.

Amelia Earhart (1898–1937), American aviator

At this point in the book, you are aware of the importance of relationships. You have a clear idea that you may have been exhibiting behaviors that were destroying trust. You have also identified behaviors that will enable you to build trusting and loyal relationships with superiors and subordinates.

The next logical step in building your career is the art of schmoozing. This is the vehicle for *how* you develop relationships. Simply put, schmoozing is the way people build relationships in business.

Schmoozing in business involves different relationship dynamics than other relationships in your life. In your personal relationships with family and friends you have a special kind of intimacy and candor. You can reveal personal experiences and thoughts. In addition, you can give your opinion, debate, and argue. The key dynamic in personal relationships is that you are frequently on the same level as the other person. That is to say, there are no hierarchical differences.

At the other end of the spectrum is networking. The classic networking concept usually conjures up images of two people exchanging business cards, with each person revealing what unique skill set he or she has. The point of the exchange is to develop leads that could advance your career. It's a very practical and business-focused transaction.

Schmoozing is different because it is done in the context of the hierarchical relationship. Also, schmoozing calls for more involvement than the typical networking connection. You've got to get to know people. They've got to get to know you. How can you know someone if you don't spend some time with them? And how can you get to know someone if you always focus on work?

Most people who do not schmooze are uncomfortable with the concept. The importance of schmoozing was completely foreign to me when I began my career. I interpreted spending time with superiors as brown-nosing, wasting time, reduced productivity, and unpractical. If I had to choose between working through lunch to get out of work early versus schmoozing through lunch, I would choose the former. Even when I saw with my own eyes that people who schmoozed got promoted and enjoyed better opportunities, more money, and so forth, I still did not understand *why* this was important. It was difficult to get motivated to participate in such activities.

What are the reasons you don't schmooze now? I ask this question in my workshops. We've got all kinds of people like lawyers, doctors, buyers, managers—and guess what? This is probably one of the scariest and most difficult subjects for any of them to address. Here is a list of the typical responses to the question: Why don't you schmooze now?

- I didn't think it was important.
- It's not appropriate.
- There's not enough time.
- If you have talent you don't need to schmooze.
- I'm shy/introverted.
- I'm not sure what to reveal.
- I'm afraid of being rejected.
- I don't like it.
- I don't want to do it.
- I don't drink alcohol.
- I don't want to be labeled.
- It's superficial.
- It's phony and dishonest.
- It feels like there must be an ulterior motive.
- I have to give up time that I'd rather use for things I enjoy.
- It's just small talk.
- It's pretending to have fun.
- My hands get clammy.
- My boss is unresponsive.
- It's uncomfortable.
- It's difficult to get the conversation started and keep it going.

- There's no rapport/encouragement from the other person.
- I'm too busy.
- I feel like an intruder.
- I feel out of the loop.
- My boss will interpret my actions as insincere or that I have an ulterior motive.
- My peers will view me as insincere.
- It's just a big power play and I'm not important enough.
- I don't like them.
- I'm afraid I might say something stupid.

There is a common thread to most of the reasons listed: shyness. There was some fabulous research done by Philip Zimbardo at Stanford University on the matter of shyness. One of his definitions of shyness is, "To be shy is to be afraid of people, especially people who for some reason are emotionally threatening."[11] He explains shyness is characterized by an excessive preoccupation with the self. We find ourselves asking questions that reflect this behavior: Will I be accepted? Will I be funny? Will they like me? Do I sound stupid? What if I make an ass of myself?

Zimbardo also discovered shyness can be situational. This means certain situations can cause you to feel introverted, even though you might not consider yourself introverted in other situations, like with your family or friends. One of the most common shyness situations occurs when we encounter people with power. Bingo! Schmoozing between yourself and a superior can be difficult because there is a hierarchical difference in power and influence.

Zimbardo describes shyness as a universal experience. He found more than 80 percent of his survey respondents reported being shy at some point in their lives. In the United States, he estimated about four out of every ten people consider themselves currently shy. Therefore, it's more unusual for you to have never been shy than it is for you to experience occasional shyness. Also, there's a good chance the person you are schmoozing with may have some tendencies toward shyness as well.

Zimbardo's research supports the conclusions that human personality and behavior can be altered. The quality of being able to adapt to different situations is the key to our survival as human beings. He dismisses the myth of the unchangeable essence, "the real me." The bottom line is that giving into shyness can keep us insulated from uncomfortable feelings of being unwanted, uninteresting, and unintelligent. To get the good stuff and get beyond shyness, you must accept you have the power to change your behavior.

If you want to become successful and experience the happiness that goes with it, you've got to be willing to take the risk and get over the shyness that is protecting you from the critical relationships you need to take you to where you want to go. No pain, no gain. Take it from me: I've had it both ways and it's worth every bit of pain to learn how to build relationships.

Zimbardo's research demonstrates shyness equally affects men and women. However, in much of the research I've come across, I found women seem to have a more difficult time understanding the importance of schmoozing. Most men will at least admit to the theory that schmoozing is important because it builds critical relationships, even though many men are shy in such situations. For the women, including my own experience, they have not even accepted schmoozing as a means to creating success.

In Deborah Tannen's book, *Talking From 9 to 5*, she notes, "Again and again, I heard from women who knew they were doing a superior job and knew their immediate co-workers knew it but the higher-ups did not."[12] This statement reflects the fact that these women who had great accomplishments were missing opportunities to schmooze and develop relationships with their superiors. They didn't understand that accomplishments alone were not enough to move them forward. And yet, they recognized they were disconnected from the power structure that could have promoted, groomed, and developed them.

When I was a little girl, my mother told me, "Karen, you are going to go to college and have your own career and you won't ever *need* a man." Like many women from the feminist era, my mother believed women could do anything. And somewhere the communication of the feminist message was interpreted to include "and you don't need a man to be successful!"

The main thing I came to realize about myself was I had developed a strong idea that I could and should be successful without *anyone's* help. I know I'm a woman, but even I have an ego problem asking someone for directions when I'm lost. I want to show the world I am independent and I can figure things out for myself. I want people to point and say, "See that woman? She is successful because she's *good!* She didn't get to where she is because of anyone helping her get there. She did it on her own."

What is remarkable is that many of my female workshop participants strongly relate to that idea. The danger in believing we can be successful on our own is that it becomes an excuse for not forging important relationships. Schmoozing is difficult because it forces you out of your protected isolation. In isolation the potential for rejection, anxiety, fear, and loss is minimized.

In Deborah Swiss' book, *Women Breaking Through*, she talks about an event in which a woman lawyer at a mid-sized law firm decided to hold an annual woman's dinner. The intent was to "counteract the absence of critical mass and to support women moving up the ranks."[13] The big night comes, and the women meet at a small restaurant that has been rented just for the purpose of their annual dinner. And guess who walks in? Several men from the law firm, including many of the women's bosses and partners. The men stayed for drinks and left when they weren't invited to stay for dinner. After leaving, they conspired with a policeman to interrupt the women's dinner and serve them with a"fake citation for engaging in 'sexist' behavior."

What is most interesting about this story is that the women felt they would deal with the night's events in the most positive way the could: They agreed to never throw it back in the men's faces at work. And that was it.

Let's take a look at this story again in more detail. First, the fact that there was limited female critical mass in the law firm was probably not a great reason to throw an annual dinner. It seems extravagant and elitist to the rest of the company who cannot attend simply because they are the *wrong* gender. If the intent was to create a support group for the women, there are many other ways to do that, such as providing mentors, workshops that address gender sensitivity issues, and so on. In that manner, everyone can benefit and participate in the effort to make the women *and the men* feel more comfortable working side by side.

Second, the very fact that the women were noticeably awkward when the men showed up is a good indicator these women were *not* comfortable socializing with the men. And *being comfortable socializing is the key to building strong relationships* that will get you promoted and recognized in the firm.

Therefore, these women need the practice of engaging in social settings to build their experience and confidence.

Third, the fact that the men *did show up uninvited* demonstrates that: Men value social time as *worth* their time. These
men were high ranking, some as high as partner, their time is
worth hundreds of dollars an hour. If they were there you can
be sure they felt it was a potential opportunity for them to
benefit. Therefore, these men actually *did respect and value*
these women in some manner, and perhaps thought they could
benefit from information being discussed, otherwise they
wouldn't have wasted their time. Also, the men believed it
was okay to show up at social events, even without a formal
invitation. The assumption is that anyone can come who
wants to. This is a good tip for women who always feel a formal invitation is required to participate. Unfortunately,
women are more inclined to have everything prearranged or
be formally invited before choosing to attend such an event.
Look at the women in this example: They set a specific date,
chose the restaurant and closed it down only to their party,
pre-selected who would be invited and who would not, and
extended the invitation.

The fourth point to this story is the action taken by the
men in persuading the policeman to serve a fake citation.
This is an attempt to use humor to "clear the air." In other
words, the men probably did feel left out, but rather than
make it into a serious issue, they used humor to send a message. The women missed a great opportunity to open up their
elite circle to the men. Instead, they chose to remain solid
and the men ultimately left. But even after leaving, they still
gave the women another chance by using the policeman.

The bottom line is this: We *need* relationships, especially
with our superiors, to help us if we are to ever move up in the
world.

At an early age boys and girls use relationships differently to reach their desired objectives. In Deborah Tannen's book *You Just Don't Understand*, she describes a videotape of three girls and three boys playing as separate groups with a plastic pickle. The children range in age from three to four years old. In the situation with the three girls, Sue determines she wants the pickle Mary has. Sue attempts to obtain the pickle from Mary by explaining a third girl, Lisa, wants the pickle. Therefore, Sue explains, Mary should give the pickle to Sue so Sue can give it to Lisa. (By the way, Lisa never indicated to anyone she wanted the pickle.) Mary attempts to negotiate with Sue by telling her she will cut the pickle in half, but Sue protests Lisa wants *the whole pickle*.

With the boys, Nick determines he wants the pickle Kevin is playing with. Nick comes right out and screams for the pickle, but Kevin declines. At that point, Nick involves the third child, Joe, and cries that Kevin won't give him the pickle to which Joe responds he can pull the pickle away from Kevin and give it to Nick.[14]

What is most interesting about these two scenarios is the way the children use relationships to garner their desires. In the first example, Sue, quite independently, tries to negotiate the pickle on her own terms. When that fails, she continues to negotiate under the guise of wanting it not for herself but for another. The bottom line is Sue is quite determined to figure out the dilemma by herself.

In the second example, Nick at first requests the toy but after failing, quickly brings in the aid of another boy, Joe, to use brute force, or at least the physical threat, to secure the toy for himself. The bottom line is, unable to accomplish a goal independently, the boy quickly engages the help of another. Just because Sue introduced her purpose was to help

Lisa, Sue did not relinquish control to Lisa. Sue stayed in control of the entire process.

This study may suggest girls may be inclined to behave more independently when pushing toward a desired outcome, even when faced with barriers. Boys appear to be much more comfortable and inclined to rely on the help (of other boys) when confronted with obstacles to achieving goals.

In the first line of Stephen Covey's Acknowledgments section in his book *The Seven Habits of Highly Effective People*, he states, "Interdependence is a higher value than independence. This work is a synergistic product of many minds."[15] That statement acknowledges the importance Covey places on relationships, and his success is built on those relationships.

At a consulting company I worked for, I observed a man and a woman, both with the same tenure at the firm, achieve promotion to partner at different times. The man was promoted to partner first. He was quite unusual from the typical partner composite, however, and it was widely regarded he had developed significant relationships with a key technology vendor that was almost half of the firm's implementation revenue. In addition, this man had developed highly visible relationships with key partners in the firm and was well liked by the partners in general. The woman, on the other hand, was leading a project at the time the man was promoted, but she did not develop any significant vendor relationships. In addition, after the project was over, she made little attempt to continue the relationship with the client. In conversation with her, I detected she may have been a little frustrated her peer had been promoted earlier than her but she finally did concede this man deserved the promotion to partner.

As it turned out she had an excellent relationship that spanned nearly eleven years with a very powerful partner.

After some heart-to-heart discussions, he helped move her from project management into technology development. She was on the road to managing a new technology practice for the firm and the critical relationships that came with that responsibility. Within one year, she was promoted to partner.

Carole St. Mark, CEO for Pitney-Bowes Business Services, understood the importance of relationships and success. After changing jobs, her boss told her the most important thing she could accomplish in her current position was to win over the CFO. Then her boss told her point blank the CFO hated her! What did she do? She figured out his needs and found a way to meet them.

In a big break, St. Mark landed an assignment the Pitney-Bowes board of directors backed, although there was little support within the company. She was completely successful in the assignment, was able to generate internal support for the solution nobody wanted in the first place, and got the attention of someone on the board who ended up becoming the company chairman. That chairman promoted St. Mark to vice president for strategic planning. Eventually she became CEO. The importance of the relationships she developed cannot be underestimated, even in light of her amazing accomplishments.

Schmoozing is important for bonding current relationships and also for building critical future relationships. The value of strong relationships is to be able to successfully leverage those relationships to become bigger than you could on your own.

There was an article in *Glamour* magazine entitled, "Truth in Beauty: The Glass Ceiling That Still Holds Back Women Hairstylists and Colorists." The premise was that men dominate the top billing echelons in the world of beauty, which puts them in prime locations and entitles them to celebrity clientele. The article stated that for years, women have explained this inequity by, "claiming that clients want to feel a 'sexual chemistry' when they're in that swivel chair. A male hairdresser's wink, shoulder rub, and sexy voice—even if he's gay—seem to matter as much as his talent with the scissors or coloring brush."[16]

Others conjecture that women place more trust in a man's idea of a sexy cut or color job than in another woman's. It is unfortunate women feel that, once again, something is out of their reach because of something out of their control. Hopefully, you know by now, there must be more to this inequity than meets the eye. Pleasantly, I discovered the article does continue: "The younger generation of female stylists doesn't accept the sexual chemistry argument. They say now, it's the quality of the cut or color service that matters—not the sex of the person behind the chair."[17] Hallelujah!

Okay, now at least we know it *is something* within our control. But we need to dig deeper. As it turns out, the men who are at the top of their profession are sponsored by major hair-care-products manufacturers. Aha! They've built alliances with the very people who can put them in a more successful position and they become successful.

The article continues to look for insights as to why men and women in the same industry approach it differently. "Men are taught to build empires," says Lisa Power, senior stylist at Gary Manuel in Seattle. "When the men enter a female-dominated arena like the hair industry, they see the possibilities of financial gain. Women by contrast, may be more inclined to feel satisfied doing something they love, even if their name is not on the door."[18] Hold on here—if women did not want to be successful, they would not be complaining about the "glass ceiling."

Having skill and talent is only a part of the whole success package. Having an ability to build relationships and to utilize those relationships is a very important part of creating success and happiness in business.

What Is Schmoozing?

Schmoozing can take many forms from an informal gathering to conversations with peers or senior management. Schmoozing usually involves the exchange of information between parties. Most importantly, schmoozing is a connection with another person.

Inherently, schmoozing is not a bad thing. It's not manipulative or something to be ashamed of. While there are many negative connotations that have been associated with schmoozing, in the truest sense of word, it's a positive thing. What could be more rewarding and satisfying than to form a mutually beneficial connection with another person?

Schmoozing provides the framework to establish a bond or connection with other people. A bond is necessary to develop strong relationships. It also provides opportunities to gain insights and information about the department/company. As your boss comes to trust you, he or she will feel comfortable revealing more to you.

Schmoozing is an excellent opportunity to share your accomplishments. In this manner you will have more visibility for your outstanding work. You can also utilize this time to voice your career preferences. If your superiors have an idea of what you want to do, they are in a better position to help you get there.

One of the best uses of schmoozing is to test the waters and build commitment. Say you have some great ideas. The only way a great idea becomes realized is with support to implement it. You need to find out if your idea will generate support.

You run it by your boss. You let your boss provide input and give you guidance as to how the rest of the department or company may view the idea. He or she helps you tailor the idea and in doing so has become committed to the outcome.

Your boss should help you identify other influential people in the organization who can help your idea become a reality. You meet with those people and run it by them, getting their input and commitment.

Don't Save Your Big Ideas for the Big Meeting

One of the important lessons I learned the hard way is to never save your big ideas for the meeting. Many people tell me they have come up with a great idea in a meeting and it was pushed aside—or worse, someone else restates their idea and seems to get credit for it.

Your idea might be good but you have weak influence over the group. Has this ever happened? You find that your ideas are barely recognized at big meetings? You find yourself getting increasingly frustrated and eventually you feel demotivated and void of wanting to participate. You finally shut down.

Kotter and Heskett define the role of leader as "aligning people—communicating the direction by words and deeds to all those whose cooperation may be needed so as to influence the creation of teams and coalitions that understand the vision and strategies, and accept their validity."[19]

If your role on the team is not leader, how does this definition apply to you? Since you are a potential influencer, which is an important characteristic of a leader, you should be interested in how to be a successful influencer of the group. This doesn't mean you have 100 percent impact with all your ideas, but it does mean you become a strong contributor to the team.

The number one action for becoming more influential with the team is to align your support *before* the meeting. Too many times I have seen people saving controversial and large impactful issues for a meeting. The meeting should be viewed as a step in the entire process of building consensus. The work begins before the meeting.

Schmoozing is an awesome opportunity to build support for your ideas *before* the meeting ever occurs. Once the meeting takes place, it becomes a formality of garnering group acceptance for your idea.

Define your position based on evaluations and rewards. In other words, what is the benefit to the team/company for implementing your idea? Select key alliances that will be important to get your idea through. Have informal discussions with these individuals on a one-on-one basis. Learn from these potential alliances what it would take for them to get behind you. Listen. Ask more questions. And finally ask for their commitment. "Joe, if we are able to find a way to increase customer service and utilize cheaper transportation such that the plant inventories would not be negatively affected, do you think you could get behind that? Great, can I count on your support in tomorrow's meeting when we discuss this?"

Be prepared that your alliances may not come through for you in the meeting. There are many reasons. There could be other factors that had not been considered previously which have great influence on the outcome. Again, since the meeting is merely a stepping stone in the entire process, utilize the time after the meeting to regroup and debrief informally with your alliances and the detractors to understand what influenced their decision.

A word of caution. It is very easy to get caught up in the emotion of being let down or rejected because people you thought would back you did not. You must get beyond that before you can be persuasive. Otherwise, all your frustration and resentment will pour out as you attempt to move forward. Let it go. As they say, you might have lost the battle but you have not lost the war. The other thing to consider is that the issues may be much more complicated than meets the eye. There could be extenuating influencing factors including political factors you need to better understand and address before you can have the kind of support you need. Remain positive, focused, and move forward.

Another tip is to ask someone to help coach you during this process. Your coach should ideally be someone from the team or the extended team. He or she should have high influence on the team and understand the issues and politics much better than you. This person can be invaluable in helping you understand the inner workings of the politics of the group. This person can guide you with respect to style, approach, and help you get to the heart of the issues. Your coach should want you to be successful.

How to Schmooze

The first rule to beginning is to remember the hierarchy is still firmly in place. This is an easy one to miss, especially if you are not in the physical work place.

A woman I know told me how her husband, Bob, made this mistake and it cost him his job. Bob was an up-and-coming attorney in a San Francisco law firm. He was ambitiously working toward partner and expected to be there within the next couple of years.

One evening, the partners and several senior associates were relaxing at a cocktail party. Bob engaged one of the partners in a discussion of Berkeley politics. Anyone from the Bay Area knows Berkeley politics can be quite controversial, to say the least. In any event, the discussion heated up to a debate. Remember what I mentioned about debating with a superior? It is not a good idea. If you are not careful, you can be misinterpreted as being disrespectful of your hierarchical differences.

The result? I'm not sure who won the debate but two years later Bob was up for partnership and turned down because the partner who had debated with him years back was voting "no." He said Bob wasn't a team player. It was devastating to Bob to lose a career-breaking promotion. He had to leave the firm.

The hierarchical status is such an important dynamic of the relationship we will spend all of next chapter discussing the etiquette in detail. One more example clearly emphasizes this point.

Johnnie Cochran was the lead attorney in the O. J. Simpson trial. Originally, however, Richard Shapiro was Simpson's lead attorney. What happened? Many years ago, Judge Lance Ito was hired into the Los Angeles district attorney's office by none other than Johnnie Cochran. In other words, Cochran was Ito's superior. Years later, Ito was the judge and Cochran was the attorney. But guess what? Ito was *still* deferential to Cochran. Many analysts of the trial said this dynamic was critical to the defense team. The defense exploited this benefit and used it to their advantage when they placed Cochran in the lead attorney position.

Always remember the context of your relationship when you are schmoozing.

Also remember to mentally move the focus away from yourself. Part of why shyness creeps over us is because we become preoccupied with ourselves and whether or not we will be accepted. Therefore, change your focus away from yourself to what the situation is all about at that moment. Think about the other person.

You will become more relaxed as you stop worrying about yourself. You will find it easier to talk and ask questions. It's natural to feel nervous. But the more you do this the easier it becomes.

It's kind of like flying. After a string of highly publicized plane crashes, I became ferosioucly afraid of flying. Just knowing I had to take a trip would start my heart palpitating and my palms sweating. When I was on the plane and it would start moving toward takeoff, I would feel myself spinning until I had complete vertigo and couldn't ascertain whether the plane was heading up to the sky or down to the ground like a bullet.

I had a job as a consultant that required me to take a minimum of two plane trips every week. Sometimes I had to take three. I realized I would die an early death if I did not do something to overcome my fear of flying.

I watched a program on the physics of flying. Amazing. I read an article about the prevalence of flying phobia in our culture. It stated the number one way people were coping with their fear of flying was prayer.

The next time the plane took off I began thinking about the scientific reasons why it would gain lift and maintain an altitude of thirty-five thousand feet. I said a quick prayer. I don't ever remember being afraid to fly again. I just stopped focusing on how scared I felt. I felt a sense of peace.

You can gain peace through prayer or meditation or any other kind of mental exercise, which allows you to relax and focus your thoughts on a desired idea. Breathing is also relaxing.

In my very first job out of school, I was scared to death of any schmoozing event that involved people with power. I will never forget the advice Bill Whitehouse gave me. Bill was the vice president of the department and kept company with all the other vice presidents. He told me I could become a reformed introvert. He began pointing out all the vice presidents who were former introverts. Somewhere along the way, those vice presidents realized they would have to become more comfortable schmoozing with people if they were to continue moving up in their careers. That gave me some hope.

What Do I Say?

My first schmoozing event was the company Christmas party and there I stood with a drink in my hand and sweat dripping down my back. I had absolutely no idea what to talk about. I looked at my manager and started discussing whatever inane project I was working on. He looked back at me and practically shouted, "Karen, it's a party! Don't talk about business!" Well, that was about it for me. I was all out of ideas.

What I have found to be especially effective is to have a flexible agenda in my head before I even go out. In other words, I already have an idea of what I'd like to talk about. That gives me a sense of security because I am prepared. Many times, only a few of the items I have prepared for will be topics the other wants to engage in. Be a good listener and recognize when the other person does not want to pursue a topic of discussion.

To become a good schmoozer, you should have interesting things to talk about. Harvey Mackay recommends the Sunday *New York Times* as being the source for everything that's interesting. There are other good magazines and reading materials to choose from. I like the *Economist* because it has social and business stories from all over the world. Books are also great subject matter. Try to incorporate into your life at least one thing that is nonbusiness–related at least once a week to keep yourself fresh. My friend has a great way of using her real life experiences as interesting stories that keep people engaged.

If it is possible, research your audience to the best of your ability. You will have more points in common to leverage, since you will know ahead of time what those points are.

Strong points of interest are things that stir up emotion:

• Alma mater for undergraduate or graduate education
• Hometown
• Sports
• Hobbies
• Armed service experience

Schmoozing should be appropriate. In some business cultures certain types of schmoozing are more acceptable than other types. I had a woman in one of my workshops explain this concept very well. She was a young, attractive woman and told of how when she took her boss out to lunch to schmooze, rumors began flying that there was inappropriate behavior happening between the two. Her boss, a happily married man with children, became uncomfortable with their relationship and began to withdraw from her.

There are many reasons such an occurrence may have happened. Most importantly, it could be that there were few women in that department and most didn't engage in schmoozing. Therefore, it was probably odd to see a young woman with her boss. You have to understand and be sensitive to the culture. In the consulting firm I worked at, the idea of a young woman and her boss having lunch would be no big deal.

If you are in a culture where one-on-one schmoozing doesn't happen, you could lead an effort to organize some team event or lunch. In one instance, I did this on behalf of the department manager, my boss. It gave me a chance to spend some time with her, connect with her vision of the lunch, and show I was loyal to her. Also, at the team lunch I was able to sit next to her and continue to build our relationship.

I was on a big ERP (Enterprise Resource Planning) implementation project and the project manager and partner wanted to throw a team dinner. This was an effort to show their thanks for everyone working so hard and to give them an opportunity to meet more of the project team.

The team had an entire dining room of a swanky San Francisco restaurant reserved. The dinner was an extravagant string of seven or eight courses. Since there were so many of us, the restaurant lined up seven long tables, parallel to each other. I watched and waited as the project manager and project partner selected the center of the center table. Incidentally, the center is viewed as the power position. Can you believe the team scurried toward the outer tables? Here was a perfect chance to develop a name-face recognition with the most important people on the project. These people could also be influential in future project opportunities. And what did most of the team do? They passed up the opportunity.

Remember Zimbardo said 80 percent of us experience shyness at some point and one of the most common occurrences is when we are in a situation with people with more power and influence than ourselves. Anyway, I knew enough to know I should take a deep breath and try to at least sit at the center table. I wasn't ready to sit *right* next to the manager and partner but I was close. It was good practice.

Schmoozing is necessary. I'm sure there are many elements of your job you consider boring or stupid but if you don't do those things you won't be able to get your job done. You don't have the luxury of arbitrarily omitting the tasks you don't like. Sometimes you can delegate but almost everyone in the world still has those unenjoyable tasks which are just part of the job. The same goes for schmoozing. You might not like it right now, but if you are going to be successful in your career, you will have to do it. Your job depends on it. Part of your job is to successfully meet your objectives. In order to do that, in some way you have to work with other people. Therefore, in order for you to be successful, you have to have successful relationships. This is why it is within your job to schmooze, since it is the vehicle for solidifying those critical relationships.

The last two things worth mentioning are eye contact and voice. One of the physical characteristics of shyness is poor eye contact. Become more aware of your eye contact, without dwelling on it too much. You will develop this as you become more confident in your ability to connect with people. Be patient and be aware of it.

If you are lacking in confidence or feeling like someone is not interested in you, you may have a tendency to let your voice trail off. I know I used to do this and I didn't even know it. A colleague pointed this out and told me he thought I was tired. That was probably his kind way of saying I sounded bored and uninteresting. Now, I am very aware of my voice in conversation. I try to speak like I'm interesting and exciting, so people will think I am worth engaging. Also, people will think I am interested in them which will keep them more engaged.

Ways to Begin Comfortably Schmoozing

There is a great book written by Harvey Mackay called *Dig Your Well Before You Are Thirsty*. It describes how to build networks of people to help you get more out of life. The one thing Mackay doesn't assume is that it is difficult to get started. After I read his book I became depressed. How I would love to be able to do what he talked about. The book should have been called *Schmoozing 400*. I needed *Schmoozing 101*.

Let's begin with the basics so you can understand how to start comfortably schmoozing. Someday you might even consider it fun!

How to Get Beyond the Fear of Schmoozing

Throughout my workshops I ask people to volunteer after each section to do a recap of what was taught. It is an excellent opportunity for people to polish their presentation skills. It never fails that about 99 percent of my classes are absolute introverts when it comes to presenting. I joke with them and support them because I really do understand how difficult it is to get up in front of people and talk.

I read a great book awhile back by Frank Bettger called *How I Raised Myself From Failure to Success in Selling*. It was written back in the 1940s. The author was pals with Dale Carnegie and they used to travel around the country giving lectures about how to do better in business. The biggest take away that I got was how this guy Bettger, became more confident in his ability to connect with people. As he became a more ambitious salesman, he realized he would have to connect with more and more powerful people, like presidents and CEOs. The only problem was he was nervous and shy. He lacked confidence. He learned how to build his confidence through public speaking.

Even after I explain the benefits of public speaking, my class will still stare at the floor when I ask for a volunteer to do a short presentation. Remember, these are smart people:

lawyers, doctors, managers. This is hard stuff, but there is so much to gain from it.

Another common problem people tell me they have is they can't get the other person to agree to schmooze with them. They feel the other person is not interested in developing a relationship with them. Now what?

The best way to make a connection is to be able to provide some value to that person, especially if he or she is more senior than you in the hierarchy. If you can't connect by virtue of your charming personality, look for something you know or have that could be of interest or provide value to the other person. Remember schmoozing is supposed to be a mutually beneficial exchange.

Another option is to ask someone who knows both of you to introduce you. You may want that person to also coach you on the best way to develop a connection with your target.

Strategies for schmoozing

Other things you can do to begin comfortably schmoozing include:

- Get to the meeting early.
- Stay after the meeting.
- Hang out in the coffee room or at the water cooler.
- Go out for breakfast, lunch, or dinner.
- Go to a sporting event.
- Slow down. Stop in and talk to people in their offices.
- Email something relevant.
- Go to a concert.
- Plan a team outing.
- Have someone introduce you to someone you want to meet (over lunch).

- Take an afternoon break and buy a cup of coffee or an ice cream.
- Car pool.

Try to come up with at least three more ideas on schmoozing in the culture you work in.

You Want to Go for a Drink?

Early in my career I interpreted going for a drink as a prelude to some kind of romantic experience. You go for drinks to meet men you could possibly date. You go for a drink with a man you are dating. When I was in college, women I knew would never go for a drink to unwind or to bond. We went to the bars to meet guys.

If we had a problem we needed to work out, we talked about it at the kitchen table. We shared our dreams and fears over Dorrito's and Diet Coke and other assorted delicacies.

There is a funny movie I am reminded of called *True Love* about two young people who love each other and want to get married. They have typical problems very young couples have and so the wedding becomes questionable. In one scene, the women in the family all sit around the kitchen table with a pie and talk about the general problems in their lives, mostly the men. The young bride-to-be is asked to sit down and have some pie and share her feelings.

Men have different social experiences and place a different value on going for drinks. Many men go out for drinks with their buddies to unwind. The drink becomes an excuse to spend some time together and connect.

If you are lucky enough to get invited out for a drink or find an appropriate opportunity to offer it as a suggestion with your manager, take advantage of the time to be yourself and the other person will begin to feel more comfortable with you. You will be thought of as someone he or she can feel comfortable with—someone he or she wants on his or her team. This is the time you want to pepper the conversations with what you have been up to. It is a much more informal and laid-back opportunity to talk about your accomplishments.

I encourage you to try this with your coworkers to get the hang of it. Find out what works for you. I say this because this was so uncomfortable for me for many years. I was very nervous with my managers and came across as awkward. This resulted in their obvious discomfort with me. I also remember having too much alcohol to drink, which made my face numb and left me questioning whether I was making bizarre facial expressions. In one incident, I became so nervous and overwhelmed I revealed to my new manager that I forgot to mention some experience I had in my resume. That was the job I got fired from, although I didn't say that, it became obvious I was trying to delicately cop to something only to quickly sweep it back under the rug.

Be careful with drinking alcohol, especially if you have little or no prior experience. The potential to overdo the alcohol is great because of the newness of the experience and your preoccupation with trying to seem relaxed. Another tip is to order a drink along with a glass of water. This way, you have a sensation you are drinking more alcohol than you really are but without the effect. I have found it can be quite uncomfortable if I am only drinking one drink and my manager is already on his second or third. Remember, if you are comfortable with yourself, others will feel comfortable and relaxed with you. You want to minimize your own discomfort.

Of course you always have option of ordering plain juice or some other nonalcoholic beverage.

I have a friend, Stacey who used to be quite the lunch-time drinker back in the 1980s and would think nothing of downing two mixed drinks before returning to her desk. She saw her health and her work begin to suffer and eventually swore off all alcohol. Now she just smiles and says, "Oh, I don't drink." That's it. The bottom line for you is to think about how you will handle the situation before it occurs so you will be prepared. Preparation will greatly minimize the anxiety and awkwardness of the moment.

Feel the Fear and Do It Anyway

When I began to realize how important schmoozing and connecting with people was for my career, I was still anxious about having to do it.

When I first wrote the proposal for this book, I met a potential agent at workshop in San Francisco. I had met her at a previous workshop and told her of my idea for a book. She was interested and told me to put together a proposal. Four weeks later I was ready to show her what I had done.

My husband accompanied me to the workshop. There were publishers, agents, writers, and retailers ready to share their stories. After the first presentation there was a 15-minute break and people began schmoozing. "Go ahead and give your proposal to that agent you know!" my husband pushed me. Wait a minute. I'm not ready. This is out of my comfort zone. Albert looked at me in disbelief, "This book is great! Go give it to her." Okay, just give me a second to compose myself. Oh, look, she's got a million people around her, she's busy, maybe at the next break.

How ironic that I'm writing about encouraging people to schmooze and I'm having to get my butt kicked by my husband to get me in first gear.

Of course I did it. I just wanted you to know it's always a little difficult for us reformed introverts. We know we'll be better for it, so we do it in spite of the fact that we don't really want to do it. You can do this.

CHAPTER FIVE

Don't Ignore the Hierarchy!

---

*Creative minds have
always been known to
survive any kind of bad
training.*

Anna Freud (1895–1982), Austrian psychoanalyst

This is probably one of the most difficult things I have personally tried to manage over my career. In the beginning, I didn't even realize I was doing anything wrong.

Much later in my career, I came across gender style communication research from Dr. Deborah Tannen that explained how women, in general, have a tendency to try to equalize positions when they speak. Women minimize the differences between themselves and the speaker. It's quite natural and comes in handy when working with groups and teams. A natural team leader is someone who can make everyone feel comfortable to contribute, regardless of level in the organization. However, this can be incredibly destructive to one's career if applied to interactions with superiors.

Dr. Tannen explains in her research that, in general, men vie for dominant position in conversation. Position is the same as recognizing a difference in status. Therefore, if women use their ability to minimize differences (thinking this will make people more comfortable), what they are *really* doing is demonstrating lack of respect for the hierarchy and frustrating the hell out of the superiors they are interacting with.

A hierarchy can be informal or formal organizational structure where there are real differences in power and influence. In other words, not everyone is equal. A person's level of power and influence can be based on the structure or independent of it. In other words, power can be perceived.

In the business culture, interactions are opportunities to establish dominance. This is a ritualistic way of reinforcing the power structure and ensuring others abide by it. The power structure itself is quite dynamic. Therefore, these interactions are very important because they serve as means to communicate the evolved power structure.

It may appear the easiest way to understand this power structure is get a copy of the company's organizational chart. This chart will reflect the formal reporting relationships. Remember, part of what we have been talking about in this book is invisible. That is, those elements of the work environment that are unwritten but are an important component of how people interact and how decisions are made. Therefore, while the organizational chart will show you who is in charge of whom, it will not tell the full story of who has power and influence within the organization.

A friend of mine, Barbara—the same Barbara from Chapter 3 who obtained a considerable salary increase at her annual review—had a terrible mishap at a previous employer that eventually ruined her career so badly she had to leave the organization. Initially she was on excellent terms with her manager, Mike. Mike had promoted Barbara back into the department after she had an unsuccessful attempt to cross-train in another department (which is another story!). Barbara came back into the department with very strong support and a good reputation.

Barbara's rank in her department was one level below her manager. Barbara only had one peer, Brian, who also reported to Mike. Everyone else in the department was a subordinate to Barbara and Brian. Now, the way Barbara tells me the story, she clearly understood that even though she and Brian were of equal status on paper, Brian was more influential with Mike. As she looked back on that experience, Barbara clearly believes Mike valued Brian at a higher level than Barbara. This is the basis from which everything will follow.

Brian was well known by Barbara and other subordinates in the department as ineffective, having poor quality work, not providing adequate support to other departments, and so on. One day Brian came to Barbara and asked her to change the work schedules in the department so he could take a more preferable work schedule for himself. (Barbara's department utilized a program called 9-80, which allows an individual to work two forty-hour work weeks in nine days, allowing the tenth day off. To provide adequate coverage, the company would have schedule A and B so that only half the work force would be off on any given Friday. As it happened, one of the schedules was consistent with all of the company holidays, allowing more four-day weekends. This was known as the more preferable work schedule.)

Barbara couldn't believe Brian was so selfish that he would unfairly ask the department to reshuffle so he could personally benefit, while someone else would inevitably lose out on a less desirable work schedule. In addition, Barbara was very surprised Brian came to her to coordinate such a task. She viewed herself as his equal and clearly this was outside of her job responsibilities.

Without another thought, Barbara went to Mike, to explain the selfish scheme Brian had improperly delegated to Barbara. Barbara explains Mike was most sympathetic to her in the meeting and nodded, showing his understanding and agreement that this was a ridiculous request. Immediately after the meeting, Barbara claims Mike began a witch hunt to demonstrate Barbara was no longer competent. She was harassed, she claims, to the point that Mike was actually fabricating evidence that she was not doing her job properly. She knew she crossed the line and once she had, there was no going back.

Clearly, even though Brian was not officially Barbara's superior, in Mike's eyes he was. Therefore, Barbara demonstrated to Mike that she did not respect the hierarchy. She showed through her actions and her words that she thought she was equal or superior in status to Brian, and worst of all, she clearly provided an example of how she would easily go over a superior's head if she didn't agree with him.

From Mike's standpoint, this should have scared the living crap out of him. How is he to maintain credibility, power, and control in the organization with someone who does not support the basic elements of the hierarchy? He was right to be paranoid.

After several months of feeling like Mike was out to get her, Barbara finally had to take some time off for medical disability. Translation: She was about to have a nervous breakdown. Indeed this was incredibly traumatic for her as she quickly saw her unique status within the organization go from special to dirt. She tried to patch things up with Mike but could not change the inevitable—the full attempt to kick her out of the organization.

While on disability leave, Barbara naively hammered the final nail in her coffin. She decided Mike was out of control and the only way to get him back under control was to appeal to Mike's boss, Steve. She composed a seven-page letter explaining the great misunderstanding and imploring Steve to become more involved with helping Mike and Barbara to resolve this unfortunate miscommunication. She made a copy of the letter for human resources. Steve graciously replied back that he would be of any assistance in the future, although the truth was he would never intervene or assist in this situation. And as Mike may have predicted, Barbara did in fact go over his head to his boss.

The day following the company's receipt of Barbara's letter, her personnel file was stuffed with loads of documentation describing her weak performance. And it just so happens, Mike provided all that documentation. If he was paranoid she was not a team player and out for her own interests, he was on the money. And her final action was merely a confirmation of this.

When Barbara returned from disability leave, Mike announced she was officially on probation unless her performance improved. If not, she would be fired in three months.

The importance of this story is to emphasize that power and influence are invisible. Understanding the organization chart is only step one. Understanding who has power and influence takes some time and observation. And don't get tricked into believing people below you on the chart are without power. A bad run in with a secretary caused a director-level candidate to lose an opportunity. The secretary had such influence with her manager, the vice president, that when he discovered a well-qualified candidate had been rude to his secretary, he was quickly removed from the list of second round picks.

As I said at the beginning of this book, I don't believe this is a problem that *only* affects women. Men actually make these same mistakes and sink their careers in the process. At a billion-dollar consumer products company, there was an exciting announcement of a newly hired vice president, who came from a larger and more successful competitor. The VP reported directly to the CEO of the company. On paper this guy looked great—he had probably more than twenty years in the very company the hiring company was trying to emulate. He had a position of power and influence. And yet after less than three years, he was asked to leave. What went wrong?

First of all, he made the big mistake of assuming the reason he was hired was to change the company's conservative culture to a more aggressive culture, similar to what he had come from. He thought changing the slower-paced culture would make the company more profitable. Over the period of time he was there, however, he did not build strong relationships with people within the organization who were lower on the organizational chart but incredibly powerful and influential within the organization. As time went by, he became less effective at accomplishing anything and soon found himself out of a job.

I think it was explained he had a difference in style from the CEO. The truth of the matter was he had not garnered the support from people within the organization who had more power and influence than he did. Without support, especially at that level, he became impotent in the organization. He was soon seen as a liability to the organization rather than an asset.

Another example involves the vice president of information technology services for a multibillion-dollar consumer product company. He was with the company for a short time and decided to influence the strategy to change technology platforms. That is, the company was a mainframe shop and he wanted to move them toward client server. A team of high-level people were organized and provided with outside consultants to help them evaluate the pros and cons of the current mainframe versus the trendy client server platform. The team finally determined that the right choice for the company at that time was the more conservative and less risky mainframe platform to run their applications. Well, the vice president was furious and hired his own team of outside consultants to explain why the company should move toward client server. In the end, his recommendation would cost over ten million dollars, while the team's recommendation would come in under seven million dollars, without the additional risk of the client server applications.

The vice president did not get the support he needed from this well-respected team that had direct contact with the CEO and board. Even though these individuals on the team were clearly below the VP in the organization, as a team, their opinions had equal if not more weight than the VP's conclusions.

The VP did not support the team's recommendation and began to act accordingly. He hired only people into his organization who had client server experience. The result was his department could not provide adequate support for the applications that were chosen to run on mainframe platforms. Complaints rose. The people who were hired into client server jobs were bored and frustrated because there was not much going on and eventually quit. The increased turnover caused the costs of the department to go up, which netted into overall poor performance for this VP.

This VP was finally asked to leave the organization. Clearly he was not viewed as a team player and was no longer seen as an asset to the organization. His department's poor performance provided the final validation he was a liability to the organization.

This is consistent with a truism we discussed earlier: Your ability to have successful relationships in the organization is primary and the ability to achieve results is secondary. That is not to say results are not important. In many fields such as in sales and marketing, achieving quotas is scrutinized very heavily and plays an important part in determining an individual's value to the organization.

My advice is to build relationships within the organization. Understand your respectful position within the organization and develop your relationships with that in mind. Simply going around being Mr. or Miss Nice Guy is not being respectful of your position. In a hierarchical organization, you cannot treat everyone the same. That is not to say you should treat anyone badly, rather you should understand your place. Are you equal in status, superior, or subordinate? That will influence how conversations are controlled.

How to Respect Your Boss
Don't do this

My earliest experience of hierarchy was a rather negative one. It was my first professional job—an internship my junior year in college. While internships have become quite fashionable now, back when I had mine, they were still relatively new. The internship was with a Fortune 500 consumer products company at a local distribution center, which was near my home. It was the first year this company had hired interns in their logistics department and it was my boss' first time supervising an intern. Needless to say, it was not very organized.

I quickly turned this downside into an opportunity. Not only did I get to do the routine office work, but I also requested and was granted the opportunity to go out with the sales reps and make calls on the grocery stores they serviced.

I got to go out in the delivery trucks and assist in making the rounds to the store docks, and I even got to work in the warehouse and help assemble store orders. I must admit even at the time I knew it was unique that I was granted so much flexibility in seeing all I saw in the operations. The first-hand knowledge was invaluable. In addition, my boss gave me a very favorable review for my time, which would inevitably be used by corporate to evaluate whether they should pursue me for full-time employment when I graduated the following year. So what could I have possibly done to screw that up?

In order for me to get college credit for my internship, I had to write a paper on my experience. I explained all I saw and did and how it better prepared me for my senior year and beyond. At the very end I expressed some disappointment the work was not always challenging and suggested the program could have been better organized. I had the stupidity to send my boss a copy of the paper. Believe it or not, I was completely shocked when my ex-boss refused to return my calls over the next year, as I wished to use him as a reference.

If you don't understand why this hurt my relationship with my former boss, let me explain. The paper I wrote was an attempt for me to evaluate the internship, and I took it to the next step and evaluated my boss's performance. Back in those days there was no upward feedback, so this was surely viewed as an act of insubordination. In addition, for all my boss did for me, he had every right to believe this was also an act of disloyalty. I had never expressed any bad feelings about the internship to his face, and what a surprise it must have been when he read a published document with negative comments. That would definitely qualify as correcting someone in public, another big no-no.

There are a couple of important lessons here. First, any negative feedback should always be given in a constructive manner, so the person understands specifically how he or she can improve. Second, the constructive feedback should never be a surprise at evaluation time. If it is, you have been remiss in your duties and must take partial responsibility for the behavior at hand. After all, uncorrected behavior is, by default, condoned behavior. Third, remember your position in the hierarchy and have a good sense to know if feedback is permitted and encouraged within the channel you seek to give it. Fourth, correcting anyone in front of others is humiliating, period.

The main problem I had was I didn't acknowledge there was a certain etiquette to follow when interacting with a superior. I thought I knew how to be respectful, but the truth was, I didn't.

Do this

The first rule of etiquette is to always let the other person save face, no matter how right you are. The best way to explain saving face is with a story.

Richard was the project partner for a big project I was working on. The situation with the client was tense. We were doing a small project, that if successful, could have turned into the largest project in the business unit. On top of that, the client was incredibly demanding and not very warm to its vendor and consultants.

Richard was the kind of person you would never imagine as a partner. He was young, fit in well with all levels of staff, and a little goofy. One day he came to work with two different shoes. He didn't even notice until someone pointed it out after lunch. He kind of laughed about it and asked each of us if we noticed he had shoes that didn't match. He had a pretty good sense of humor and ability to laugh at himself.

On another occasion, Richard caught a morning flight to the client site. The plane had a lot of turbulence and he ended up getting doused with coffee. All over the front of his pink oxford was a huge coffee stain the size of three loaves of bread. He was embarrassed when he got to the project because he had an important meeting with the CFO and Richard knew he looked ridiculous.

One of the guys on our team saw Richard and in an effort to help Richard save face said, "Hey, Richard, I see you're wearing Starbucks' logo today." As consultants, we frequently wore our client's logos to show our loyalty to them. Since Starbucks was an actual or pending client, it was a cool statement to make. Just the same, it gave everyone the opportunity to laugh, including Richard. Richard's pride was firmly intact.

I worked on a project with a manager who was incredibly difficult. Matt would constantly change direction with the client and neglect to inform me. I had to work with senior personnel and ascertain where our position was from feedback I got from them. This proved to be a very frustrating experience. It was difficult to plan, it was difficult to direct the team I managed since our course kept changing, and eventually it was very difficult to stay motivated because there was just so much uncertainty we eventually felt as if we were only spinning our wheels, going nowhere.

I began to write in a journal during this period because I was so frustrated and knew there was no one in the organization with whom I could share these feelings. I had a good friend who was having similar issues working for the same boss, and we would get together and laugh about how difficult it was to work for Matt. But I primarily relied on my journal to capture all the petty little things Matt did or did not do and how angry and frustrated I was becoming.

Eventually, I was able to clear away some of the emotional stuff and boil the situation down to three critical issues that would essentially put the project at risk. I practiced those points and reviewed them with Matt. In addition, I had a coach within the organization and I reviewed the specific issues and required steps to be taken to improve the situation. I documented our conversation and asked for guidance as to how to proceed. He encouraged me to work through the situation with Matt directly.

This was a difficult time, but I was careful not to share my explosive emotions with my coach. I knew he could end up defending me should things fall apart on the project, so I wanted my coach to have a clear, unclouded view of how I methodically evaluated the situation and the steps I took to deal with it. In addition, I knew it couldn't hurt to let on that I was remaining optimistic and appreciated his support during this challenging time. That way I was able to build confidence in his mind that I was capable of dealing with difficult people and situations. I was building my image as a strong leader. Meanwhile, I was crying to my journal on a daily basis as to what an idiot Matt was and the latest round of things he had or had not done to make my life difficult.

The payoff was unbelievable. I was able to remain in very high standing with Matt, who until this day thinks of me first when selecting top people for a visible team project. In addition, I was able to get assistance from my coach on how to finally bring the big issues up to Matt's boss, without alienating Matt. My coach did some preparation for me by having some informal discussions with Matt's boss about his concerns on the project. This way Matt's boss knew there could be some problems and would not be blindsighted. Also, this allowed me to protect my position by not appearing to go around Matt in an effort to protect my own self-interests, which would have surely portrayed me as not a team player, disloyal, and out for myself.

When things had gotten to the point of stop or go, I received support and encouragement from my coach to jointly inform both Matt and his boss of my impressions and a firm recommendation. I did this through an email. In addition, because I had a clear focus on what the main points were, my memo was unclouded by emotion.

A key tactic I used was allowing Matt to save face. I structured my recommendation on disbanding the project based on some key events and feedback I had received that were well beyond Matt's control.

The result was Matt could no longer object to disbanding the project. What was interesting was a couple of weeks later Matt's boss called me asking me for feedback on what was happening with the project. Apparently he never read my email. He asked me to be candid and said our conversation was "off the record." How I would have loved to tell him what an ineffective manager Matt was and how the project nearly failed because of Matt, but I quickly decided this call was not a progress report on Matt's performance.

Instead, I shared my observations and repeated my conclusions from the original email. I was careful to state that it was only my opinion, so he could draw his own conclusions. He disagreed with some of my opinions, but I was very careful not to debate or try to persuade him into thinking my way.

The result from this was a powerfully positive performance review and recognition from both Matt and his boss. No bad will was created and I have strong credibility with both Matt and his boss. I have since had the opportunity to make recommendations they were eager to support.

Giving Up the Last Word and the Conclusion

Did you know another way to show respect is to allow the other person to have the last word? Not giving up the last word can be an insidious form of insubordination because you don't even realize you are doing this.

I frequently found myself giving the last word on a discussion because I found a point of disagreement with my manager. I thought it was important that if I didn't agree with him I should restate my position. What I learned is that by allowing the other person to have the last word you are actually respecting his position and not necessarily agreeing.

The last word is an important concept that took me over a decade to understand. If you allow your superior to have the conclusion, it does not mean you agree with your superior. I would find myself summarizing a conclusion of the conversation to give it closure. What I was really doing was showing I was uncomfortable with my position in the hierarchy, which I was.

When I had begun to understand this concept, I was immediately tested on a project with a very opinionated project manager. It was clearly obvious the project manager was ranked higher than I was because of his status and experience. Therefore, what was most helpful to me was knowing that when we engaged in almost any topic he felt he was the expert, I gave him control of the conversation and let him determine its conclusion.

My role was to listen, learn, and occasionally offer my viewpoint. I did this most delicately as in, "I can see your point. In my opinion I see things this way...." I was very careful not to get into a power struggle with this manager. He had the unwritten privilege of having the last word on any conversation. Period.

This manager would try his hardest to ruffle me. Once he started one of our lunch conversations off with, "Hillary Clinton is a bitch. What do you think?" Personally, I don't believe that but I was quite aware that my position was not to defend, persuade or criticize. So, I carefully took a deep breath and answered, "I've heard many people say that. But I happen to think she's been a good source of energy for the White House and here's why . . ." I had respected my boss' opinion without losing my integrity and agreeing with him. We completely disagreed on the subject matter but were still able to maintain our respective positions in the hierarchy.

Occasionally, I found he would entertain a topic in which I had much more knowledge than he. And he would actually defer much of the conversation to me by asking, "How does this work?" However, I came to understand my position was clearly subordinate and even after collecting much information from me, if he still differed in opinion, he got to conclude the conversation with his final words.

This may sound really stupid, but I was immensely rewarded for my behavior. It turned out my physical contribution to the project was minimal. However, when this manager reviewed me he gave me an incredible evaluation, stating specifically I was unexpectedly easy to work with. I know I can directly attribute this perception to respecting his position and deferring control and conclusion of the conversation to him. While I can admit to you those conversations were at times difficult for me, I do understand the purpose was not my entertainment. In other words, you debate and explore ideas with your friends and your significant other, not necessarily your boss. In the work place, conversations are frequently used as a gauge to see if you understand your position in the hierarchy and if you respect others.

Be Careful of Accepting the Conclusion —Know the Right Answer First

Once I was working with a partner on revising a proposal. We had already presented the proposal to a particular company; it had been well received and now we were being invited back to give the same presentation to a higher level of management. Unfortunately, the project partner insisted on revising every page, every line, and every word of the document.

This entailed working past midnight and huge extra efforts by other staff. There was a tremendous level of effort, cost, and exhaustion required from people to refine a document that, in my opinion, really did not require any revisions, at least not to the degree the partner insisted.

At the end of the period, we finally went into production of the document and the partner asked me and my colleague for our feedback on the new and improved document. I was completely caught off guard, and so very confusedly I said something about it being fine. I was pretty unconvincing, and the next day the partner reminded me I didn't sound sure of the revisions last night. What did I think now?

Overnight, I had time to think about and discuss this with my husband. I remember telling him, "Can you believe the nerve of this guy? He spent hours and loads of money revising a perfectly good presentation and he asks me if it is any good? It was good 3 days ago!" My husband, ever so delicately, reminded me it really doesn't matter what I thought of the presentation, because in the end it was not my responsibility for the success of the presentation. It was my boss's direct responsibility to ensure the presentation was successful. Therefore, my job, he reminded me, is to ensure my boss feels good about what he is crafting, and I will ultimately support whatever he develops.

Back in the boss' office getting ready to answer his question about what I thought about the final presentation, I turned to my boss and replied, "you are the leader on this presentation. You have much more insight than I do on what is required to make this presentation win. If your gut tells you this is the direction we should take on this, I know it is the right thing to do and I will support you. I feel good that we have a presentation that will be successful." His reply? A smile, and no more discussion on the subject.

The bottom line was that it was after the fact. The presentation was completed and no feedback would really change it. So, the course was set and I had a choice: get on board and support it or criticize it. I'm a team player and got on board. We eventually did win that work.

Pushing Back Versus Challenging Authority

What if you need to tell your superior something difficult? You realize the right answer is not something your boss may want to hear but you know it is in your boss's best interest. Your ability to push back and not challenge (and to understand the difference between the two) will confirm you are loyal and committed to your manager's success. Therefore, this type of behavior can build or destroy your credibility as someone who is loyal.

Pushing back refers to your role as an "advisor." It is not as confrontational as "challenging," but it does mean you are questioning the direction set before you. Another way of looking at this is in terms of coaching. Coaching is input you provide with the intention of helping another to develop and ultimately reach their goal. If your intentions are misread as self-motivated, you run the risk of being seen as "challenging" rather than coaching. Therefore, select the situations very carefully in which you wish to push back because you always run the risk of being misinterpreted.

A couple more thoughts on this subject. You might be thinking if this is such a touchy subject, why even run the risk of being misinterpreted? I'll just keep my mouth shut and follow orders. Well, there is something to be said for being a "yes man," but for most of us this would not be satisfying.

When my husband was just starting out, he worked as a paralegal for a lawyer who did not want to hear any ideas from his support staff. This lawyer would shoot off orders and expect them to be followed without any further discussion.

My husband, Albert, would sometimes notice there were negative legal implications in proceeding verbatim with the lawyer's instructions. Albert would attempt to renegotiate the lawyer's demands, only to find an angry and frustrated delegater who was not the least bit interested in Albert's ideas. Finally, Albert was completely frustrated and said, "Listen, I understand how you want this done but I have some ideas I want you to hear. I have a brain and I think and I can't just take orders from you like a machine. If you don't like what you hear, you don't have to do it, but at least give me the opportunity to participate, because I can't work like this anymore." Well, the lawyer was surprised to say the least, and he gave Albert a minute. He listened and said, "Okay, I've heard what you said. Now do it my way." Without any hesitations, Albert did what he was instructed.

It wasn't critical to Albert to change the outcome; it was important he was able to have input in the process. Eventually the lawyer saw Albert was very bright and came to actually take some of his advice once in a while.

My experience has shown me the more intelligent and the more of a *true leader* your manager is, the more you can benefit from developing his trust that you are someone who can provide excellent coaching. Yes, that's right. You can provide excellent insights your manager can benefit from. Let's discuss how.

Because of your position in the company, you may see things your manager might not see. You may understand the complexities of operations better than your manager. Therefore, you have the insights that might be invaluable in making or modifying business decisions. Pushing back is the act of explaining (as an advisor) why something cannot be done exactly the way your manager wishes. Let's explain this in more detail.

First, the assumption is that a business decision has been made, is going to be made, or is being discussed with you. Second, you have some special insights as to why that business decision should not be made entirely the way it is being made. Third, you can articulate those insights and also provide options that could still allow the manager to reach his or her objective. I always refer to these other options as plan B and plan C. That way it takes away your personal ownership (as in "my idea") and transfers it to no one. Fourth, there is valid cause for you to go to the trouble to even intervene with the business decision. Don't move to intervene unless you really believe your manager can benefit personally. Remember, whenever you intervene in a decision, it could be interpreted as manipulative or unsupportive. Therefore, chose carefully where you should invest your energies.

One of the most difficult interventions I ever did in my career was telling my immediate manager that he should resign from the project I worked on for him. There had been an abrupt change in client management on the project team and the new client project sponsor had on more than one occasion made a public spectacle of my manager. The longer I thought about it, the more I believed the new sponsor's actions were personally motivated.

Strategically, my manager had tremendous influence within the client project sponsorship, which existed of several people, including the CEO and the former CFO. It was obvious this new sponsor was threatened by my manager's influence and sought to remove him. My manager had just been part of another proposed project that was flatly turned down by the new sponsor, during which the new sponsor derailed the presentation and took shots at my manager.

In order to preserve the longevity of the project I was working, I determined my manager must remove himself at least publicly or face cancellation of the entire project. I believed that up to this point, my manager did not see the big picture and did not fully understand how badly his relationship with the new client sponsor was affecting our current project.

I found myself sitting in my manager's office and explaining to him I thought he was doing an awesome job managing a difficult transition with the new client sponsor. He showed incredible professionalism and patience and I really admired him for it. (I was very sincere in my praise.) I explained I had some genuine concerns for *his* project, in that I felt that based on what I had seen and heard, the new sponsor continued to act in a hostile manner to him. Therefore, it wouldn't be much longer before the new sponsor closed the entire project down. This project was my manager's main responsibility and he needed it to be successful no matter what.

I recommended that in order for the project to be successful, my manager should publicly resign from the team. The benefits of doing this would redirect the new sponsor's anger away from the project, which should at least allow the project to be successful, since it had strong support internally. It would also provide additional time for my manager to develop more—and potentially more—lucrative business leads within the company, by leveraging his influence. It would eliminate much of the day-to-day stress my manager was currently facing having to deal directly with the new sponsor.

My manager listened and agreed with my logic. He asked me what logistics would be involved with transferring project management responsibilities and I shared a list of tasks with him I had already drafted in advance of our discussion.

First things first, he had to get his management's approval to do this. He agreed to get back to me before the end of the day on next steps. He was very grateful and thanked me very much for my insights and support. Clearly, I was trying to help him survive and excel in the process. I did not want to see him go down in flames. After discussion with the project partners, my manager did not end up taking any of my advice. My bottom line was unchanged, however, and that was to make my boss successful. If he was going to stick out what I thought was an almost impossible proposition, I would do anything I could to make it possible for him to be successful.

In summary, the "formula" for pushing back is as follows:

1. Acknowledge your manager's vision *and* your support for it.

2. List your concerns but intersperse your commitment for the vision.

3. Explain your recommendation and *how* it can benefit your manager and *how* it supports his or her vision.

4. Get out of the way. No matter what your manager decides, it is his or her right to make the "wrong" decision. Remember your job is to support and help get him or her to the finish line.

5. Tell your manager you support him or her. If you can explain how you will be able to support from the restated position, do it. (This might be plan B.)

To my knowledge, using this formula, exactly the way I have explained it, has never resulted in a negative backlash from a manager. As I said earlier, it can actually build confidence and trust between you and your manager and reinforce your perceived loyalty and commitment to his or her success. This is the key to future promotions, more money, and better opportunities for you.

Another approach that is often confused with the push back is challenging authority. When you think you are being totally reasonable and logical, your behavior may actually be challenging, thereby destroying trust with your superiors.

Alex was awarded the opportunity to bring in his boss and some additional people on his sales team to present to a large client. A key contact, with whom Alex had a very good and long relationship, was the primary inroad to this presentation at the company. The key contact requested Alex's agenda in advance and wanted to know who was to present what. Because of my experience presenting to big accounts, Alex asked me whether or not this was standard practice.

I told him it was. The more important the time of the people we are presenting to, the more critical it is that we get input and sign-off from the client on our agenda. This allows us to better develop our presentation, since we will be able to tailor our sales presentation so it goes like this: "We think we may be able to help you...here's how." It comes off as less of a sales presentation and more of a friendly conversation targeted toward their business problems.

Alex's immediate boss was outraged when Alex recommended client input on the sales presentation. His boss shouted, "What if they don't want to hear what we have to say? This gives them the opportunity to say no. You should have never done that!"

Alex, completely frustrated and annoyed by his manager's misplaced logic, said his boss's argument did not make sense. Collaboration with the client could only be an advantage.

Since Alex was telling me the story, I decided it was okay to give him some input. I asked, "You didn't really *say* that to your boss, you just *thought* that, right?" He said, "Of course I said that."

I said, "Look, your boss has a valid point, and it probably deserved to be addressed. His concern that some of your sales talk may be shot down before you even get there is absolutely within the realm of possibility. I would have handled it a bit differently. I would recommend that you first acknowledge the fact that his concern is a valid risk. Building on that, state your experience as proof that in these situations you have benefitted more from knowing some key insights into the problems of the client and therefore, have been able to tailor the presentation. It may help you avoid topics they are not interested in right now. The bottom line is you have seen this type of approach build loyalty with the key contact because he is convinced you are trying to make him successful and will gladly open more doors in the future. On top of that, because you have your key contact support and key insights to the company, you have additional credibility when you speak at the presentation."

The previously described story may be an obvious form of challenging authority, but there is another type of situation that is much less obvious but much more detrimental, because in many cases you don't even realize you are doing it. I will explain this by telling you another story about Alex.

In his business, Alex helps his clients produce bakery products. He sells them the mixes (or "bases" as they are called in his industry) and they mix them with water, form the goods on trays, and run them through their ovens. Sound like a simple process? Actually, it's incredibly complex. Alex is highly knowledgeable and understands the intricacies of oven temperature; the speed at which trays pass through the oven; the amount of water, temperature, and humidity in the bakery, which varies by time of year; and a host of other factors as well.

When Alex's clients want to minimize their costs and maximize production, he finds their shortcuts often produce undesired effects in the baked goods. Alex will approach a situation by first listening to what his client wishes to do. Knowing full well that if the client produces the product the way he just described, a lower quality product will be produced. Alex says, "Okay, that's one way you could do it. Here are some other options to consider.... Or if you don't feel those work for you, you could always do it the way you just described." The result is that most of the time the client responds angrily, "Oh, so, you don't like the way I'm doing it?"

Alex told me this story and said he doesn't understand why if he delivers his suggestions in a totally civilized manner, he receives such an "uncivilized" response. Clearly what was just described was not pushing back but challenging authority. Clients, who have higher status, can ultimately do whatever they wish. Alex did not acknowledge what the client's objective was and instead cut right to the chase and told the client he could do it like that or do it his way. This resulted in a challenge of the client's authority, or his ability to act as he wishes.

Simply put, the client does not believe Alex is interested in his interests. The client probably thinks Alex has a big ego and is only concerned with his own way of doing things. Alex didn't even stop for a minute to explain why doing it the client's way could result in an undesired outcome. In addition, Alex assumed his objective was the client's objective. Alex's objective is to produce an A-plus baked good, which is probably different than the client's objective: to produce a B-minus product but do it quickly and cheaply (willing to trade off the quality of the final product for savings in time and money).

A good question to ask before you determine if you are pushing back or challenging authority is: Do I understand what my manager's objective/vision is? If you are making an assumption, and especially if it is based on your own objective, stop and ask, What are you trying to accomplish? What is the objective of this decision? Help me understand what is the vision or big picture of what you are doing? If you are met with any resistance, I bet it is because you probably have challenged his or her authority in the past. It may take a few tries to build new trust. In any event, confirm your new interest by stating, "If I can understand what you want, I can be better focused on making you successful and reaching that objective." Again, depending on your past experiences with this person, you may have to work a bit to build some credibility, so be careful to act consistently with your words.

Once you understand what your manager's vision is, get behind it. Acknowledge you believe in it and support it. If you cannot personally support such a request, I strongly recommend you find another manager or job. Since this is a component that is fundamental to loyalty, you must believe in your manager.

Therefore, the whole notion of challenging authority really is just a subset of pushing back. In other words, challenging authority is just the recommendation. It is truly amazing how much less of an impact your recommendation will have without the recognition and alignment of vision and an explanation of concerns. The recommendation should be the last and least important in your agenda. I always ask permission to give a recommendation. This will ensure the audience is open to feedback and minimizes the risk of being viewed as insubordinate.

Sometimes there may be overriding political reasons why some business decisions are made, even if you have insights, those insights are not going to have an impact on the final decision. Even if you proceed to list your concerns, when you get to the point where you ask permission to give a recommendation, you may still be turned down. I have frequently been given an explanation as to why it is not worth the effort to explain my recommendation but many times I received none. There is nothing wrong requesting such insight but I caution you to keep your ego in check. If you think sour grapes may reveal themselves don't question the refusal.

Another example shows how quickly a moment of challenging authority can turn into a decision to expel one from the team. A friend of mine, Linda, was a full-time teacher in San Diego. She taught low socioeconomic multicultural students who had a history of not being model students. Linda is herself a product of a low socioeconomic multicultural family and felt she was able to connect with the students in a way ordinary teachers could not. Her program was so successful her principal constantly invited teachers and principals from all over the country to observe Linda teach her class. Linda had what she considered a very good relationship with the principal, who was a woman.

One weekend, Linda realized she was pregnant by a man she had been living with for a while, so on the spur of the moment, she decided to tie the knot. Her boyfriend was delighted as he had been asking her to marry for quite some time. That weekend they were married. On Monday, Linda told her principal she had married that weekend and by the way, she was pregnant. The principal responded rather harshly and scolded Linda for marrying too young (she was twenty-nine). In the faculty meeting that followed, the principal announced Linda was married and pregnant. Linda was completely shocked that the principal violated her privacy by making such an announcement.

In any event, things for the most part continued as they had. Linda continued to teach and receive recognition for her unique program. She did harbor some hurt and angry feelings about what she felt was inappropriate behavior by her principal. About three months after that incident, Linda requested time off for the Jewish holidays, which were two months away. Specifically, she requested two days off for Rosh Hashanah and one personal day on top of that. The principal replied, "I thought Rosh Hashanah was only one day?" Linda replied, "No, it is two days." The principal responded, "Well my calendar shows it is only one day." Linda responded, "Well your calendar is obviously not a Jewish calendar, because it is wrong."

The principal said she would only give Linda one day off for the Jewish holiday and she would not grant her the personal day. Shortly thereafter, the vice principal began to sit in on Linda's classes and provided very critical feedback about what was wrong with the class. Linda sensed she was being set up to get fired and she called her union representative. Off the record, her representative found out the vice principal was indeed told to sit in on Linda's classes and to try to find what was wrong with her program in order to get her fired.

Linda ended up not taking any time off for the Jewish holidays in a last-ditch effort to repair the relationship with the principal but to no avail. Her realization of how bad the situation was had begun to sink in, so she decided she would seek employment elsewhere. In addition, she told her union representative she did not want to file a complaint against her principal because she didn't want to get a reputation for being a troublemaker.

What is most interesting about this story is Linda actually *had gone against her principal* when Linda told her she was wrong. Linda challenged the principal's authority by declaring the principal had the wrong calendar and insinuated Linda's calendar was the one that was correct. Another level of interaction that may be difficult to see in these pages is the fresh hurt and anger Linda was still carrying around from the earlier incident where the principal inappropriately announced Linda was pregnant and married. Linda might have held that second fateful conversation with a "chip on her shoulder" that came across very loud and clear as defying authority. In other words, Linda might have felt, *you got me once, but I'm not going to let you win this one!*

When Linda demonstrated she was more self-concerned than committed to the principal, the dynamics changed very quickly. The principal realized she did not want Linda on her team. This is most interesting because we clearly see the principal did not just become neutral to Linda; she took action to have her removed. And also note that Linda was giving the principal national recognition with her unique program of teaching difficult students, but in the end that did not matter either. Loyalty and commitment had been replaced with an antagonistic attitude, which resulted in the decision to get Linda fired.

Probably what is even more fascinating about this incident is Linda's final analysis of it. She believes the reason her principal was going to get her fired was because Linda requested too much vacation time at once. To this day, she still believes this to be true and so is careful to never take more than one day off in her current position. What is unfortunate is that like Linda, most people would probably conclude the reason this situation occurred is because of things *outside their control*. Linda recently gave me a footnote to the story and said she later found out the principal was rumored to be anti-Semitic and *that's why* she might have overreacted to her request for time off. While that is indeed a possibility, I still strongly believe that Linda's confrontation was enough in its own right to get her kicked out.

Don't Ask Too Many Questions

This is probably where I have made the most mistakes early on in my career. Over and over again I alienated myself with this technique and had no idea of its impact. After realizing it was not my position to make the final business decision, I somehow determined I could show my deference to the team or my superior by addressing my concerns in the form of a question. For instance, say the team was talking about what to do for the Christmas party. My questions would go something like this:

- "Well, what about the people who don't celebrate Christmas? They might be offended."
- "What about our big department quarterly meeting, scheduled for the same day?"
- "What about people with dietary concerns?"
- "What about spouses?"
- "Open bar may encourage people to drink too much. How should we handle that?"
- "What about a gift exchange?"

All of these questions are good things for the group to consider in planning the annual Christmas party. However, what you have done by raising these questions is associated yourself with the problem. The objective of the team is to build consensus and reach the objective. If you constantly derail the effort to reach the objective by throwing obstacles (questions) in the way, you are no longer a team player. Anyone who has worked in teams knows how excruciating it can be to develop consensus and get things done. Therefore, a true team player is committed to helping the team reach the stated objective. By asking questions and raising issues, you are a problem creator.

I used to think that by asking the questions, I was showing my submissiveness to the group or my superior. I thought this was a good thing. I thought I was demonstrating I did not believe or try to assert power over the final decision. I also thought I was adding great value because I had key insights to complex issues.

This error in analysis was pointed out very strongly by a former captain in the marines, Eric. We were working on a project together as a team and we began to brainstorm the next steps. I began to raise what I thought were excellent issues to be considered with any actions we decided to take. I did this in the form of many questions. Finally, I could see Eric growing increasingly frustrated with me, although I really didn't know why and he yelled out, "What do *you* think we should *do?*" To which I meekly replied, "I don't know, that's why I raised the question." And he shouted back at me, "Yes, you do know! What is your recommendation?" After being taunted in front of the whole team, I felt compelled to offer my idea to the group.

Eric was right, though. I did know the answer, that's why I asked the question. I felt if I came right out and said, "We should do XYZ," I would be perceived by the team as being too pushy, or worse yet, trying to exert power over them. In the case of a superior, I would be nervous of coming off as insubordinate.

I am not sure why I thought asking questions was a submissive means of having some influence on the outcome, but I've seen women do this more often than men. It may be the way women are socialized and girls are taught to be less direct. In any event, I can tell you it seemed the most natural thing in the world, and I was completely surprised to learn it had the opposite impact I had intended. By asking all those questions and rarely providing a possible solution, many of the men actually felt I was manipulating them! Therefore, they felt I was wielding power in an unwelcome manner. This definitely accounted for the high level of frustration I encountered.

The lesson here is don't be part of the problem, be part of the solution. If you have a good reason why the group or your boss should take or modify an action, first ask yourself:

1. Is it a petty or minor point? If it's petty, maybe you should keep it to yourself. There are many difficulties in building consensus in teams, so don't derail the process unless you have good cause. In regards to your manager, it is equally difficult to build consensus and align people in the organization to take action, therefore, if you get into too much detail over minor issues, you may actually appear unsupportive. Therefore, pick your issues carefully and don't be such a perfectionist.

2. If it is an issue that definitely needs to be considered, what are the impacts of not considering it? You should know these before you even proceed as you may be asked to defend your point. This is where I think women actually have a stronger advantage over men. Many studies have demonstrated women and men think differently—men think linearly and women think circularly. The implications are that women can understand multiple implications and consequences much more quickly and more naturally than most men. Therefore, a woman may have to take care to explain the intricacies of her issues in a manner that is easy and simple for everyone to follow. My favorite example is cause and effect. That is a pretty linear relationship, therefore, most can follow it.

For example, the team is planning the Christmas party and you realize the company had very poor earnings that year and in your experience, poor performance usually means toned down Christmas parties or in some years, they are eliminated altogether. Therefore, the cause is the poor earnings and the effect is a scaled-back Christmas party. Keep the relationship simple and avoid personalizing it too much or getting defensive.

3. The issue is important and you understand the impacts of not considering it, so what is your recommendation? This is your attempt to recommend a course of *action* to remedy the issue. Again, I would strive to keep the recommendation brief and to the point. If you start going off on tangents, you will lose your audience and potentially your credibility to solve problems. Try not to use this as an opportunity to throw a half-developed idea on the table, hoping someone else will take the responsibility for resolving the issue. The most important thing here is to come across as understanding the issue and being part of the solution. If we go back to the Christmas party example, you may develop a resolution by recommending the team find out what other departments are planning for their parties. Since the economic performance of the company hasn't been wonderful, maybe a scaled-back party or one combined with another department's is more politically correct and respectful of the company's hard times. Your recommendation should be short and clean in terms of the relationship of what you are suggesting accompanied by a brief "why."

Your issue passes all the criteria above, so now it is time to voice it. Be very careful here, because this is where I have watched many people fall apart. We can have a tendency to feel instantly defensive about our point so that is how we end up presenting it. This is a surefire way to damage your credibility so be aware of your emotions.

Listen to Yourself

One of the big boo-boos I have made and watched others make is letting a lot of emotion creep into the voice when expressing a point of view to a superior. I have also watched as most, including myself, almost immediately lost credibility and became impotent in persuading.

The first, and probably most common, example is when you are already frustrated and the tone comes across as "I am frustrated, I have a really good point, and you are such a putz if you don't take my advice." This can also come across as condescending, which can be interpreted as insubordination or disrespectful of your position in the hierarchy.

It also can be interpreted as losing your cool, which may be viewed that you don't handle stress very well, which can be further interpreted as you are *not* promotion material.

Many people will put up with a situation hoping it will change. Unfortunately, the expectation is things *will* change and when the expectation is not met, frustration, resentment, and pain develop. These strong feelings build every day. We begin to rehearse in our head what we would say to resolve the situation, should an opportunity to speak present itself— that is, we get the guts to express how we *really* feel about the situation.

Finally, some opportunity does present itself and we find ourselves expressing the very thoughts we had rehearsed for several days, weeks, or even months. The amount of emotion required to get these thoughts out is very high, and so the listener not only gets your ideas, but all your pent-up emotions as well. Granted, sometimes these can be subtle and other times they can be much stronger.

My advice is to first practice the fine art of detachment. Detach yourself from the outcome. When you set your expectations, you set yourself up to be let down and become frustrated if things don't work out the way you plan. Therefore, cut out the expectation and you avoid the pain later. Sounds simple, but this does take a fresh approach.

I found that because I was very goal oriented, I naturally developed expectations along the way. I didn't differentiate between the goal and the *expected* outcome, like roles, performance, opportunities to participate, and so forth. So when my expectations of the outcome were not met, I found myself extremely critical of how things were handled and very frustrated.

I have successfully avoided this later on in my career by deferring to my manager as to how things will be handled along the way. I offer recommendations based on my experience, but I have no expectation that my manager will accept any of my ideas. Whether or not my ideas are accepted and acted upon has shown to be irrelevant in terms of being in good favor with my manager and getting opportunities to grow in my career. My focus is always on supporting his final decision. Period. He knows I am loyal and I will see to it that whatever course of action is selected I will do everything within my power to make it happen. Once the manager has made the decision, the time for collaboration is over. Now is the time for action.

As I discussed earlier, no one should align him- or herself with someone they don't respect on some level. You probably won't agree with every strategic move your manager makes, but in the end, you should feel he or she tries to do the right thing, has some excellent qualities in some area, and will reward your loyalty. If you have determined this criteria is not or cannot be met, it's time to start planning your next career move.

What's In It For Them?

The second example is using reasons to persuade your manager to do or not do something. Usually these reasons speak to the heart of the matter and on a level that is not tied to the manager's objectives. Your manager should have some clear objectives, such as minimize inventory investment, increase productivity, and so forth. These objectives should coincide with your manager's criteria for evaluation and reward. If you understand this, you can begin to develop powerful leverage in your ability to persuade and influence.

Using the evaluation/reward criteria, you can now structure your suggestions within the framework of how doing something will be beneficial to your manager or how not doing something could be harmful to your manager. Remember, keep the passion and emotion in check whenever presenting. Too much emotion can destroy your credibility and leave you impotent to influence, even if you have made an excellent point.

My frame of mind when I get ready to make a recommendation is that I have an idea I think may make my boss/the team even more successful. If you truly believe that and feel it, you will convey it. When I get ready to speak, I may ask for permission to make a suggestion if I am unsure of the team's momentum. That is, if the team has closed a subject and is moving on to another area, they may not want to reopen the former subject. As I mentioned before, building consensus is very difficult so take extra care not to derail this process too often and then only when it really matters.

I often present my idea as a recommendation and preface it with the phrase "this is my opinion." In that way, I am demonstrating that I am sharing my perspective but I am *not expecting* the team or my boss to act on my recommendation. This is a very important distinction. If you truly are sharing your burning issue because you *expect* the team or your boss to follow it, you should reconsider even making it. That is, you are now officially wielding power that is probably not welcome. If you don't get your way, you will ultimately be very disappointed and hurt. By expecting the outcome, you may also motivate your audience to do the opposite of your recommendation, simply because they wish to show you who is in charge (and it's not you). So avoid these power struggles and be clear about detaching yourself from the outcome.

Deference Does Not Equal Equality

I had a personal experience of misunderstanding hierarchical relationships with one of my first female managers. Every week we had a one-on-one review session to discuss progress and issues on the state of things. In an effort to connect with me, she minimized our differences and began to speak to me like a peer. I must say, I felt very comfortable talking to her about my thoughts and feelings. I confided some complaints, like the feeling that certain men I worked with were unreasonable. We laughed and I felt we were really bonding. I remember knowing when she was pregnant before she did. I just had a weird feeling and sure enough she was. Talk about being in tune with someone.

I felt I had a really good relationship with my manager. She knew what I thought about things, I knew what she thought about things. We complained about the same jerky people and I would tell her what I would really want to say to those people if I didn't have to be so professional. We laughed and I genuinely enjoyed her company.

My first review came and I was completely shocked that many of the things I told her about how I thought about things now came back to haunt me. There were some of those very insights on my review! Wait a minute, that's how I thought but that's not how I acted. I was always professional and courteous to everyone I worked with. It became obvious my thoughts were actually being critiqued in the review and now I regretted I had become too comfortable with this manager.

In the same period, a close friend of mine, who was a peer working for the same boss, also had the exact same thing happen to her. She had trusted her manager and shared her true feelings, and they came back and resulted in a disappointing review.

My friend and I both agreed we had genuinely enjoyed sharing our thoughts and feelings with our manager and felt good we could be so honest. It was a very satisfying feeling to connect with a superior in that way. But we lost sight of the fact she was also our superior and had the responsibility to evaluate our performance. By telling her our feelings and thoughts, we developed negative impressions in her mind as to how we really related to difficult people and dealt with problems. And the proof was in the evaluations we received.

The moral of this story is to be on your guard against superiors trying to minimize differences with you. You want to provide them with the best possible picture of your abilities and work habits. You don't want to cloud and confuse their impressions with negative intangibles like how you feel about something. This is a general rule of thumb, or I'd-rather-be-safe-than-sorry rule. I have found that sticking to the fact, rather than how you feel is much less risky. Especially when your feelings are very strong and emotional.

Dress Code and the Hierarchy

The dress codes can be as invisible as the hierarchical culture they exist within. Understanding and *respecting* the dress code is a clear indication you understand your position within the company. And the more hierarchical the structure, the more emphasis will be placed on conforming to the dress code.

I remember my first corporate experience out of college. I went to Macy's and purchased my first work suits. I bought a bright blue suit, a light tan suit, a blue and white herringbone, and a traditional double-breasted black suit. All consisted of a tailored skirt, just an inch below the knee, and a fitted jacket.

One day I wore my light tan suit with a silky, long-sleeved, high-collared cream blouse. I looked very professional and feminine. I always got compliments on that suit. However, that day, the vice president of the department saw me and commented I was wearing a brown suit. The conversation went something like this:

"So, Karen, you are wearing a *brown* suit today."

"Yes, Bill, it's one of my favorites. Isn't it nice?"

"Well, it is *brown*."

"But it's a nice brown suit. I always get lots of compliments on it."

I used to joke around a lot with the vice president. So I thought he was just joking around when he started commenting on my clothing. What I later found out from him was that he purposely pointed out "bad" clothing choices to all the staff. Most of his targets, however, had always been men. He would ensure that the ties worn were consistent with his perception of the dress code. Believe me, you would never see a bright flowered tie in that department!

In addition, he also kept the general appearance of the suits in check. He told me it was absolutely unacceptable for a man in his department to wear a brown suit. I believed that when he saw me in my suit, he jokingly gave me a hard time. I just hadn't realized that to him my wardrobe choices were in the same category as a man's suit.

Another example happened early in my career. It was a horrendous day, complete with snow, sleet, and a windchill that made it feel like your head would freeze. As I got dressed in my cold apartment, I couldn't bear the thought of going outside into the tundra with only high heels, stockings, and a skirt. So I dusted off a pair of very nice gray dress pants, matched them up with a pretty cream blouse, and a fitted double-breasted black blazer.

I had a feeling pants would probably not be appropriate, even though they were very nice dress pants. I just couldn't recall any of the women wearing slacks in my department. That morning several women commented on my pants. They were very positive and supportive. I know I was feeling slightly guilty so I appreciated all the good feedback. Then the vice president caught sight of me out of the corner of his eye.

"*Pants!* You are wearing *pants* today?!"he exploded.

"That's right! Do you know how cold it is out there? It's not fair you men have the choice to wear nice warm wool slacks while we women have to freeze in a little skirt or dress with the wind and snow blowing up our exposed legs!" I said, half seriously and half laughing.

I don't think I suffered too badly because I had a sort of joking relationship with him. However, this experience, once again, made me very aware of the dress code. I always dressed conservatively and received positive comments from people at all levels, both male and female.

As a footnote to that story, after the women in the department saw I was able to wear dress pants and "get away with it," most of the other women began wearing pants too. It was like a counterculture movement silently taking place.

My best advice to you, is to keep your ears open and listen to comments that are made regarding how you dress. It's easy to take negative feedback personally, since so many of us dress to express ourselves. In business culture, the dress code is just a means of showing your connection to the team. Play within the bounds of that dress code to show you are a loyal team player.

Ask for feedback in a nonconfrontational manner. I have had good experiences asking for a check on my style to make sure it was conforming to expectations. For the most part, I have found you can't go wrong if you dress a little bit nicer than the dress code. For instance, if there is a business casual dress code in place, most of the men will wear khakis and an oxford or polo shirt. I recommend women wear dressier slacks, shoes with a bit of a heel (if you can), and something more feminine like a sweater or blouse on top. I believe clothes can be power, so I always took the opportunity to dress as well as I could without standing out like a sore thumb.

It is also important you dress within the means of your respective department. In other words, if you are wearing obviously fancier clothes than your managers, you could appear insubordinate.

My friend had an interesting experience at her office. She works in a very hierarchical company but her immediate department is all women. My friend's and her husband's combined salary is substantially more than any of her immediate supervisors' incomes. Consequently, my friend has a killer wardrobe, great jewelry, and drives an expensive car.

Unfortunately, she has seen the consequences of her good fortune turn bad in her work place. Her supervisors pick on her and make fun of her dress as in, "Gosh, don't you ever wear the same thing twice?" My friend has said it is so uncomfortable, she must "dress down" to the office style of dress. She tries to minimize the amount of jewelry she wears to the office. She's even toned down her makeup and hair to appear more simple.

The lesson here is that you should take precautions to dress in context to your superiors. The quality and style of your clothing should not overshadow that of your managers. To overstep this boundary is to confirm you do not respect your position in the hierarchy, you are not a team player, and you are not dedicated to your supervisor. This act of disloyalty could make you a prime target for removal if the opportunity should arise, in addition to poor work assignments and reviews.

Your Peers Are Your Equals

It never fails that I get questions about the peer group, even though for many of us, this is the easiest relationship to master in the work place. It is a relationship characterized by equal hierarchical status. Sometimes, however, this relationship becomes a superior-subordinate relationship and that's when the real difficulty begins.

It is very common when you are new to a job or a department to seek out friends, allies, and coaches. Be careful! A common mistake people make is using a peer as an expert on the issues and politics of the organization. That move essentially pushes your new-found peer into the superior position and you into the subordinate position.

Everything goes along okay until you've decided you're up to speed and don't require the services of this person as a superior any longer. You try to establish more of a peer relationship, since after all, you are equal in status. The fireworks start to fly and every time you have an interaction with this person you find yourself completely frustrated. What's going on?

This can be extremely dangerous for your career, as exemplified by a woman I know. Tina began working in a new company and quickly built some wonderful relationships with top management. In addition, she found a peer in another department to coach her along during her transition period.

After a couple of months, Tina felt pretty knowledgeable and up to speed in her position and so began to pull back from utilizing her peer as a subject matter expert. The peer resisted. The relationship had been formed and there was no way this peer was going to allow Tina to show disrespect to her authority.

As Tina began to show less interest in her peer's recommendations, which were appearing more as orders, the peer began to publicly pick away at Tina's credibility. She would openly cut down Tina's ideas in meetings. Tina was completely baffled. What did she ever do to set this woman off to wanting to destroy her?

One of the telltale signs you have violated your position in the hierarchy is a public attempt to destroy your credibility by your superior. What the superior is trying to do is to symbolically push you back *down* into your respective position in the hierarchy. The superior will whittle away your ideas, your credibility, and eventually your confidence in an effort to make you subordinate.

Tina's peer was actually showing Tina she had violated their relationship. Since the relationship had been established as a superior-subordinate relationship, this was the relationship Tina had to deal with.

My friend, Ginger, was hired as a graphics designer reporting to the president of a small but growing international freight forwarder. There was one other person who worked in her department. Mike was an exempt employee, while Ginger was hourly. However, the president, Bob, assured Ginger from the beginning of her employment she was equal in status to Mike.

After a few weeks, Mike started noticing the boss was giving Ginger many other tasks that were somewhat secretarial in nature, so Mike also began delegating administrative tasks to Ginger. At first, Ginger was frustrated but did what was asked of her. She told me, "Bob said Mike and I were equal, so how does Mike have the nerve to use me as his secretary?" I asked her why she did what Mike was asking her and she just responded that she didn't know.

I reminded her that her objective was to make her boss, Bob, successful. If Mike needed help and that would help the team, it was okay to help him out. However, if Mike was trying to change the nature of their relationship and subordinate her, it was *not* okay.

Like any situation where the person you are dealing with does not understand his or her respective role, it is *your* obligation to coach them. If we had received that kind of coaching, we wouldn't be learning about the concepts in this book. We wouldn't have made so many mistakes. You get the point. This is your obligation now.

I said to Ginger, "Look, you've got to coach Mike and let him know he is your peer. You work for Bob. You are loyal to Bob. If Mike needs some help, like any good team member, you'll pitch in, because you all share the same vision: Make the boss successful. Let the emotion go. There is no need to feel angry at Mike. He is testing your relationship. It's natural for most men to vie for dominance in their relationships. You *can* control this relationship. Your boss has given you clear direction. All you have to do is start acting and thinking consistently with your respective position."

My friend started rehearsing this speech in her head. Initially it was peppered with a lot of profanity since she was about ready to kill Mike. After about a day, she felt all the negative emotion gone. She began acting differently with

Mike. She felt confident in the nature of their relationship and her actions were consistent.

Mike never delegated another task to her again. My friend felt good and no longer frustrated. And the weird thing was, she never had to even *tell* Mike her speech. Her actions, even the way she began speaking to Mike, were clear indicators that she viewed their relationships as peers. The vagueness was gone. Mike acted accordingly.

Acknowledge You Need Help

My friend, Olive, is one of the smartest people I know. She graduated at the top of her class in dental school and went on to become one of four people in the country selected to participate in post-graduate periodontal study at an elite school. The program's director, Steve, had personally hand-picked Olive and was very excited she accepted the opportunity to study in his program.

The first year of the program was great. Olive was learning a tremendous amount since the school was leading the world in technology and surgical techniques.

As her second year approached, Olive began to realize a couple of things. First, she was incredibly knowledgeable. Part of the program required her to read just about everything that was being published on the subject of dentistry. Her capacity to understand and memorize thousands of articles was truly amazing. Second, Olive was a very skillful surgeon. As she advanced in her practice of procedures, she noticed her technique was superior to many of the other students, including the seasoned professors. This led Olive to her final conclusion: I know more than everyone else.

It was during her second year that Olive's relationship with the director, Steve, had become so bad Olive started seeing a psychiatrist and began taking an antidepressant drug.

Olive told me Steve was so mean to her she couldn't tolerate being in his presence for even a few minutes. If it wasn't for the drugs, she would have probably suffered a mental breakdown.

I asked Olive what she thought the problem was. She began telling me what an egotistical creep Steve was and he was just the most difficult personality in the world to deal with. I asked her if she thought he was smart. She said yes. I asked her if she thought she was *smarter* than Steve. She said yes. "Okay, that's your problem," I told her.

Olive's view of the world changed after her second year. Initially, she was there to learn. Everyone knows a little more than she did, was her attitude, and she needed them to help her succeed in the program. By the second year, she saw she had surpassed everyone in knowledge and skill and no longer needed help. It was beyond her capacity of logic to think of a reason as to why she still needed Steve, the program director. Soon her actions and communications became consistent with her feelings of superiority.

Steve was sensing Olive's insubordination and began to treat her accordingly. He publicly attacked her, her ideas, and her techniques. He was trying to push her back down to her place in the hierarchy by blowing some of the steam out of her ego. Olive continued to resist and the attacks got worse. Finally, she went into counseling and on medication.

This story has an amazing ending. Olive was able to revive her relationship with Steve back to what it had originally been. Here's how she did it: She became more subordinate in her behavior and communications with Steve. She did this by asking for his help. She asked him how he might consider solving a problem, or his opinion on a medical question.

The bottom line is that you don't have to *require* help to ask for it. Asking for help acknowledges that you need your boss to be successful. This doesn't mean you can't do anything without asking for help. Also, be careful to limit the types of things you ask your boss to provide input on. You don't want to end up rewriting an entire report or changing the entire strategy of a project. Remember, people feel important when they get to be the subject matter expert. Always show your respect for your boss and give him or her the opportunity to help you.

Say Thank You

The last yet certainly not least way to show respect is to acknowledge others who have helped create success and happiness in your life. The relationships you build will hopefully last for years to come. Many people will do a little for you but some will do a lot. Be good enough to remember them with a handwritten card, a bottle of wine, a box of cookies, chocolates, or flowers. People have long memories of who hurt them and who was kind to them. Always make it a point to be the latter.

Learn From
Your Mistakes

A great tip I learned about the power of making mistakes is that to make the mistake is not necessarily to learn anything. A great example of this is getting a ticket for speeding. Does that mean you will never speed again? Probably not. So how can we profit from our mistakes?

First, is to recognize you goofed up. Don't beat yourself up over it. This is a waste of time. And simply telling yourself you will never ever do *that* again doesn't work. The very action of trying *not to do something* makes it that much more likely you will do it.

Second, begin to analyze what happened. Who was involved? What were your intentions? What was the impact of your actions and words? How did your actions and words cause the undesired outcome?

Third, determine if this is behavior you *need* to correct. This can be difficult, and I recommend the use of a coach. Sometimes we do or say things that will have an uncomfortable impact. While we don't enjoy these types of experiences, sometimes they are necessary. Therefore, we must not always assume because a situation has been difficult we have committed an error. One thing I have learned is there might be an opportunity to improve the delivery of the message to soften the unpleasantness of the situation. Bottom line: There is always some room for improvement.

Fourth, now that you have determined you want to change your behavior, decide what the substitute behavior will be. This is much more effective than simply relying on the affirmation that you will not do that thing anymore. This way you have a clear vision of what successful behavior looks and sounds like.

Fifth, with your coach, practice what that substitute behavior is. Get feedback on your new message, tone, sincerity, and eye contact. Now you will know what successful behavior *feels* like.

Sixth, practice, practice, practice. Find opportunities in your life to demonstrate the new behavior. If you don't use what you have learned you may lose it. In some instances, it may mean there are preventative measures you can take to avoid the uncomfortable situation you recently found yourself in. Therefore, maintain proactive behaviors whenever you can.

Earlier in my career, I maintained a clear focus on what *I* thought was important. Therefore, whenever I got a request from anyone else to do something outside of my focus, I felt annoyed. I probably did not do a very good job concealing my annoyance and consequently, many of these other people quickly learned to work around me and without me. This left me out "of the loop" of opportunities that could have been fun, interesting, and visible. I decided this was not a desirable outcome.

My substitute behavior was to answer my phone or a face-to-face request for anything with, "How can I help you?" Quickly, I was able to see the benefit of offering to help. I became open to more opportunities and began to make some nice social relationships on top of that. Now, that is not to say I violated a previous rule by helping everyone with everything. I was still able to maintain some ability to push back work. But now I was perceived as easier to work with than earlier in my career.

It is not the mistake we learn from; it is the careful reflection, analysis, and eventual change in behavior that can help in avoiding repeating past mistakes.

Which brings me to the Appendix of this book. This brief summary of resources available to help you in the work place is something I wish I had early in my career. I have read all of these wonderful books, and I can assure you each has some pearls of wisdom from which you may benefit. I highly recommend you read as much as you can and remember to share and give something back to the other people you meet in your career who are as clueless as you were before you began this path of enlightenment. It is your obligation.

The Final Words

I wish I could give you a magic pill that could make all your experiences in your career wonderful, but unfortunately no such confection exists.

Many of the tried and true elements of getting ahead in the career track still ring true today: Love your work, work hard, and get the credentials you need to be successful. Hopefully, you understand that to make it all come together and create abundant success and happiness you've got to make the investment and develop strong relationships with your superiors.

In the end, we are all connected by the same thread of love. Deepak Chopra said when you reject others, you are really denying your own acceptance. To accept another is to add to your own self-love. Relationships guide us into accepting others for what they are and ultimately accepting ourselves, warts and all.

This is a hard road, but it's worth the pain. I am living proof of that. I wish you all the joy, happiness, and success you endeavor to create.

~ NOTES ~

1. Paul Witteman. "Men Will Be Boys," *Time*, volume 143, number 15 (April 11, 1994): 67.

2. Peter King. "Bad Blood," *Sports Illustrated*, volume 80, number 14 (April 11, 1994): 36.

3. Deborah Tannen, Ph.D. *You Just Don't Understand*, New York: Ballantine Books, 1990, page 32.

4. Stephen R. Covey. *The Seven Habits of Highly Effective People*, New York: Fireside, 1989, page 238.

5. Jim Morrison. "At Bat at Last," *Spirit: Southwest Airlines Inflight Magazine* (April 1998): pages 44, 112.

6. Peter King. "Bad Blood," *Sports Illustrated*, volume 80, number 14 (April 11, 1994): 36.

7. Ibid.

8. Jack McCallum. "Scorecard," *Sports Illustrated*, volume 80, number 13 (April 4, 1994): 20.

9. Peter King. "Bad Blood," *Sports Illustrated*, volume 80, number 14 (April 11, 1994): 41.

10. Paul Witteman. "Men Will Be Boys," *Time*, volume 143, number 15 (April 11, 1994): 67.

11. Philip G. Zimbardo. *Shyness*, Reading, Massachusetts: Perseus Books, 1977, page 13.

12. Deborah Tannen, Ph.D. *Talking From 9 to 5,* New York: Avon Books, 1994, page 136.

13. Deborah Swiss. *Women Breaking Through,* Princeton, New Jersey: Peterson's, 1996, page 22.

14. Deborah Tannen, Ph.D. *You Just Don't Understand,* New York: Ballantine Books, 1990, pages 44–45.

15. Stephen R. Covey. *The Seven Habits of Highly Effective People,* New York: Fireside Books, 1989, page 9.

16. Lisa Kovalovich. "Truth in Beauty: The Glass Ceiling That Still Holds Back Women Hairstylists and Colorists," *Glamour* (May 1998): 116–121.

17. Ibid.

18. Ibid.

19. John P. Kotter and James L. Heskett. *Corporate Culture and Performance,* New York: The Free Press, 1992, page 98.

How to Succeed in Business Without a Penis: Secrets and Strategies for the Working Woman by the beautiful and comical Karen Salmansohn. (Harmony Books, New York, 1996)

If you have ever read any of Karen's books, you know she has a dazzling sense of humor and wit that will make you laugh aloud. The reason I think this book is one you should read is because first of all, Karen takes the stand point that there are no victims here. Yes, it may not be a quick snap of your fingers to get you to where you want to go, but if you have faith, you will get there. She encourages the reader with real-life experiences. She was quite accomplished at just twenty-something as a senior vice president for an advertising firm in New York, only to give it up and become a writer. She knows about making it and has a great perspective on what we women need to think about as we determine what it is we want to be successful at. She gives some very good ideas on getting started with determining your special purpose and also wonderful tips on building and maintaining self-confidence, which is truly the foundation for any success. At some point, *you* have to believe *you can.*

Karen talks about the natural abilities and qualities we women can claim. In addition, she cautions the reader that like any strength played to excess, these advantages can quickly turn to disadvantages. A good insight that too much of any good thing can be a bad thing. I promise you after reading this book, you will be inspired you *can* and you will not hate men.

What Your Boss Doesn't Tell You Until It's Too Late: How To Correct Behavior That Is Holding You Back by Robert Bramson, Ph.D. (Fireside, New York, 1996)

Dr. Bramson has counseled countless men and women who were either sent to him by management to get a better personality, or were willing participants who knew their current personality was holding them back. He doesn't spend any time telling us *why* we do certain things. His belief, for the most part, is many of us can benefit by simply understanding we are doing something that is not making our lives happy.

The good news is that Dr. Bramson is able to provide us with clear descriptions of the process involved in changing one's behavior. The bad news is, once you are labeled, he notes, this is very difficult to undo. However, he has one of the most excellent examples I have ever read about how someone was able to get promoted using the help of enlisted supporters. This example of utilizing strong relationships to succeed in an environment that is not supportive to attaining a promotion is worth the money you will pay for the book.

That's Not What I Meant! How Conversational Style Makes Or Breaks Relationships by Deborah Tannen, Ph.D. (Ballantine Books, New York, 1996)

This is required reading for anyone who has to open his or her mouth to communicate. Dr. Tannen is educated in the study of sociolinguistics. She explains that she chose this career after the breakup of her first marriage. She was at first motivated by the desire to understand *why* it seemed that she and her husband could not communicate.

Something to keep in the back of your mind as you read is there is a mixture of all types of communications here. Communications between intimate friends, lovers, workmates, and bosses should each be considered in their own right. Within the context of the different relationships, certain types of communication may be appropriate while with other relationships, the same type of communication may obviously be inappropriate.

What is absolutely fantastic about this book is that it provides insights to how we communicate and the style by which we convey meaning. It is the meaning beyond the verbal message that can make an otherwise simple exchange complex. Dr. Tannen is quite capable of making the technical terms easily understood by us nonlinguistics.

The Mafia Manager: A Guide to the Corporate Machiavelli by V. (St. Martin's Griffin, New York, 1991)

This book provides some unique perspectives into management. The author explains the importance of loyalty, sponsorship, and the politics of the hierarchy. My favorite chapter of all is the one on soldiers and lieutenants that provides some more important insights to loyalty. V is able to get to the point and cover all the bases with fewer words than most. Therefore, out of deference to V's style, I will keep this recommendation short and to the point: unique insights that will enlighten your perspective of corporate politics.

Roger Dawson's Secrets of Power Negotiating by Roger Dawson. (Career Press, Hawthorne, New Jersey, 1995)

This book contains an awesome body of knowledge for anybody who has to negotiate for anything. One of the problems we have is our ability to safely ask for what we think we deserve and get it. Without sexual delineation, Roger Dawson, gives us the proven steps involved in making the most of negotiations.

I personally benefitted from Roger's tactics when I negotiated my starting salary at a new job. I increased my salary by 49 percent—but that wasn't even the best part of it. I later learned

I had come in at the top of the range for that position and that my salary was equal to and also higher than men at that level of status. The playing field was leveled. Thank you, Roger!

And if that isn't proof enough, my husband, a lawyer, has also used Roger Dawson's techniques in his own practice of negotiating with clients and insurance companies. The results have been incredibly satisfied clients and very large settlements.

Becoming a Manager: How New Managers Master the Challenges of Leadership by Linda A. Hill. (Penguin Books, New York, 1992)

When I was interviewing for my first manager position at Hewlett-Packard, I remember making it through several rounds of interviews quite easily as potential peers and superiors poked around at my technical skills and experience. I seemed to nail even the most difficult questions. On the next round, I was invited back to meet with a manager in human resources. Over lunch, she asked me about my management skills. I told her how I had successfully implemented a program, even though I worked with many different types of people, even very difficult ones. She asked me to explain my ability to work with different types of people, especially difficult ones. I quickly and sincerely replied that I just treated everyone the same. (Obviously, this was well before my knowledge and respect for hierarchical relationships.)

As I was relating the story to my husband he shook his head in disbelief. I thought that demonstrated how fair I was. No, it clearly demonstrated I didn't know what being a manager was. Different people should be treated differently. Well, he was right, I didn't get the job. But I did pick up a copy of Linda Hill's book.

This is a great book because it gives some insights as to the primary role and purpose of *being a manager*. It is highly recommended for becoming a manager or becoming a better manager. Either way, if you plan to move up, you should understand what will be critical to your success.

You Just Don't Understand: Women and Men in Conversation by Deborah Tannen, Ph.D. (Ballantine Books, New York, 1990)

In this book, Dr. Tannen focuses on the difference between men and women in conversation. When I originally read this book the first time, I remember I kept saying aloud, "Oh my God." It was like a light bulb went off in my head. I learned why some of my seemingly benign exchanges had erupted into a pissing contest, in which I always lost (even if I thought I won).

Dr. Tannen is also able to help us understand why men communicate differently than women. What is it about our socialization, even though we grow up in the same family, that produces different styles of communication? She also provides excellent insights as to the power struggles we engage in, not even knowing we are doing it. After all, she explains, conversation is but one avenue to establish and reinforce position and status. Therefore, the more insight we can have into understanding what constitutes position and status, the better prepared we can be in relating. Hopefully, this will allow more opportunities to be better understood and minimize the experiences of miscommunication.

Interestingly enough, as I read this book I couldn't help but notice I seemed to possess many of the male communication style generalities and fewer of the so-called feminine ones. That, in an of itself, at times did help me to be a better communicator with men, however, in the end, I still needed the framework within which men operate. Because even though I could "speak the language," I did not understand the context within which I was communicating and found there was still tremendous opportunity to be misunderstood.

I think this is one of the best books Dr. Tannen has written on the subject of men and women and conversation. If you can only choose one book to read, I recommend this one.

The Seven Spiritual Laws of Success by Deepak Chopra. (Amber-Allen Publishing and New World Library, San Rafael, California, 1994)

This may seem an unlikely addition to your library of what to read to improve your work relationships and communications but I assure you it is well worth the time.

Deepak explains the importance of freeing yourself from your ego. What I have found in my own personal experiences, is that most of the time when I am acting inappropriately, it *is* because my ego has gotten in the way. He explains how to keep your ego from getting in the way and where you should be focusing instead.

This pleasant little book is one I find myself reading over and over again. It has clear explanations of each behavior and a short mantra at the end of each section. I keep it by my bedside and open it up to read just a chapter every now and then. It has provided me with guidance and reminders of why I want to be a better person and also the detailed steps on how to do it. That's always been an acid test for me on the practicality of a self-help book: does it tell me *how* to get there? You may find this book has far reaching impact, not just on your career but also on how you relate to people in your personal relationships as well as with yourself. It's an inspirational book for everyone.

The Working Woman's Legal Survival Guide: Know Your Workplace Rights Before It's Too Late by Steven Mitchell Sack. (Prentice-Hall Press, Paramus, New Jersey, 1998)

Sack is an attorney devoted to employment law and has counseled many female clients. The book was "written to give women the edge."

Sometimes we may find ourselves in difficult situations because we are women. Sack is able to clearly outline what is within bounds and what is out of bounds for employers. He does this in a way that is easy for nonlegal types to understand. In addition, he organizes his book very logically, which allows it to be used easily as a reference book.

Sack provides steps you can take if you feel your employer is overstepping boundaries and how you can prepare your lawyer, if that course is warranted. The other thing I really like is that Sack explains what *is* and *is not* legal. True, sometimes it is a bit of a gray area, but having the line in the sand at least gives a framework to work within. For instance, if an interviewer asks you what your address is, that is legal, but if the interviewer asks if you rent or own your home, than it is an illegal question.

And if go to a lawyer you must, Sack provides great tips on preparing for that encounter, including what to expect, what arbitration is, and even how to improve your chances for a favorable arbitration award.

Dig Your Well Before You're Thirsty by Harvey Mackay. (Currency Doubleday, New York, 1997)

Harvey Mackay is the most lovable salesman you would ever hope to meet. From the moment you pick up this book you know he knows exactly how to successfully build relationships. Mackay is the president of an envelope company and a bestselling author. He has built a strong network of influential and powerful people who have helped in every aspect of his life including getting his first book published and getting on *The Larry King Show*, to buying the right house in the right neighborhood.

The message you should see consistently as Mackay shares anecdotes is that in order to build relationships you have to have something to offer. And the more you have to offer the more likely you are to be able to connect and successfully leverage a relationship.

If you read my book already, you know how important relationships are to create a happy and successful career. Therefore, I would recommend skipping the first four chapters of Mackay's book which explain why it's so important to build relationships.

Also, keep one thing in mind as you read Mackay's book. He has been successfully schmoozing for over thirty years. Many of us are just beginning to jump into this so it still feels overwhelming. Take what you can from his experiences and remember you will evolve over time and your level of comfort will gradually increase as you become more experienced and confident in your ability to build strong professional relationships.

The Seven Habits of Highly Effective People: Restoring the Character Ethic by Stephen R. Covey. (Fireside, New York, 1989)

This internationally bestselling book is a landmark for the work place and emerged at the end of the 1980s after a decade of greed and overindulgence. Covey appropriately subtitled the book *Restoring the Character Ethic*. Covey's message is simple as he explains how our relationships should mature from dependent to independent and finally to interdependent.

Covey shares anecdotes to make the relationship lessons more concrete and interesting. In addition, Covey shows the interconnection between the quality of the relationships we develop and the quality of the life we create. He provides very powerful and timeless lessons that are beneficial at any career stage.

How to Survive the Loss of a Love by Melba Colgrove, Ph.D., Harold H. Bloomfield, M.D., and Peter McWilliams. (Prelude Press, Los Angeles, 1976)

I originally read this book after a serious relationship breakup that left me emotionally devastated. This book is also appropriate for other types of emotional loss such as those related to career and work. Many of you who picked up my book may be in a crisis or have just left a bad work situation. *How to Survive the Loss of a Love* is an excellent book because it breaks down the process of grieving and healing into short one-page chapters. Beside each concept is the most beautiful and painful poetry that perfectly expresses the point.

It's another tool for you as you progress in your development. And you may find other uses for it too.

Man's Search For Meaning by Viktor E. Frankl. (Simon & Schuster, New York, 1959)

This is simply the most amazing story I have ever read. Every motivational or inspirational seminar, book, or tape series will make some mention of this book because of the incredible lessons in the human spirit.

Viktor Frankl was a young psychiatrist when the Nazis arrested him and sentenced him to a death camp. This is not another depressing story about what happened during the Holocaust. Rather it is the story of the survivors and how hope and love and purpose enabled resistance to disease and extreme conditions.

Frankl almost didn't write this book. It was only after the prodding of friends that he acquiesced, but he stated he would only publish it anonymously because he did not want the book to earn literary fame. At the last minute he gave in to his friends who urged him to lend his name to the work to establish credibility. And so he did.

The reason I'm recommending this book as part of your library is because it is the framework for why you exist. Your purpose and the meaning you give to your life is what makes getting up in the morning worthwhile. Many people, when faced with a career meltdown, lose their direction and sense of purpose. It's good to have a tool to help you get back on track by separating what matters from what doesn't. That's why I wrote this book and that's why I've dedicated my career to helping others build successful and happy careers.

~ REFERENCES ~

Bettger, Frank. *How I Raised Myself From Failure to Success in Selling.* New York: Prentice-Hall Trade, 1992.

Bramson, Robert. *What Your Boss Doesn't Tell You Until It's Too Late: How To Correct Behavior That Is Holding You Back.* New York: Fireside, 1996.

Carnegie, Dale. *How To Win Friends and Influence People.* New York, London, Toronto, Sydney, Tokyo, and Singapore: Pocket Books, 1936.

Chopra, Deepak. *The Seven Spiritual Laws of Success.* San Rafael: Amber-Allen Publishing and New World Library, 1994.

Colgrove, Melba Ph.D., and Bloomfield, Harold H. M.D., and McWilliams, Peter. *How to Survive the Loss of a Love.* Los Angeles: Prelude Press, 1976.

Covey, Stephen R. *The Seven Habits of Highly Effective People: Restoring the Character Ethic.* New York: Fireside, 1989.

Dawson, Roger. *Roger Dawson's Secrets of Power Negotiating.* Hawthorne: Career Press, 1995.

Frankl, Victor E. *Man's Search For Meaning.* New York: Simon & Schuster, 1959.

Hennig, Margaret and Jardim, Anne. *The Managerial Woman.* New York, London, Toronto, Sydney, Tokyo, and Singapore: Pocket Books, 1976.

Highman, Edith L. *The Organization Woman.* New York: Human Sciences Press, Inc., 1985.

Hill, Linda. *Becoming a Manager: How New Managers Master the Challenges of Leadership.* New York: Penguin Books, 1992.

King, Peter. "Bad Blood," *Sports Illustrated,* volume 80, number 14 (April 11, 1994).

Kotter, John P. and Heskett, James L. *Corporate Culture and Performance.* New York: The Free Press, 1992.

Kovalovich, Lisa. "Truth in Beauty: The Glass Ceiling That Still Holds Back Women Hairstylists and Colorists," *Glamour* (May 1998).

McCallum, Jack. "Scorecard," *Sports Illustrated,* volume 80, number 13 (April 4, 1994).

Mackay, Harvey. *Dig Your Well Before You're Thirsty.* New York: Currency Doubleday, 1997.

Morrison, Jim. "At Bat at Last," *Spirit: Southwest Airlines Inflight Magazine* (April 1998).

Sack, Steven Mitchell. *The Working Woman's Legal Survival Guide: Know Your Workplace Rights Before It's Too Late.* Paramus: Prentice-Hall Press, 1998.

Salmansohn, Karen. *How to Succeed in Business Without a Penis: Secrets and Strategies for the Working Woman.* New York: Harmony Press, 1996.

Swiss, Deborah. *Women Breaking Through.* Princeton, New Jersey: Peterson's, 1996.

Tannen, Deborah Dr. *Talking From 9 to 5.* New York: Avon Books, 1994.

Tannen, Deborah Dr. *That's Not What I Meant! How Conversational Style Makes or Breaks Relationships.* New York: Ballantine Books, 1996.

Tannen, Deborah Dr. *You Just Don't Understand: Women and Men in Conversation.* New York: Ballantine Books, 1990.

V. *The Mafia Manager: A Guide to the Corporate Machiavelli.* New York: St. Martin's Griffin, 1991.

Witteman, Paul. "Men Will Be Boys," *Time,* volume 143, number 15 (April 11, 1994).

Zimbardo, Philip G. *Shyness.* Reading, Massachusetts: Perseus Books, 1977.

Give the Gift of

Don't Sabotage Your Success!
Make Office Politics Work
to Your Friends and Employees

CHECK YOUR LEADING BOOKSTORE OR ORDER HERE

❑ YES, I want _____ copies of *Don't Sabotage Your Success! Make Office Politics Work* at $14.00 each, plus $3.49 shipping per book and 99¢ for each additional book (California residents please add $1.15 sales tax per book). Canadian orders must be accompanied by a postal money order in U.S. funds. Allow 15 days for delivery. International orders please add $11.00 for S&H for the first book and $7.00 for each additional.

❑ YES, I am interested in having Karen Ginsburg Wood speak or give a seminar to my company, association, school, or organization. Please send information.

My check or money order for $_____ is enclosed.
Please charge my: ❑ Visa   ❑ MasterCard
                    ❑ Discover ❑ American Express

Name _____

Organization _____

Address _____

City/State/Zip _____

Phone_____ E-mail _____

Card # _____

Exp. Date_____ Signature _____

Please make your check payable and return to:
Enlightened Concepts Publishing
P.O. Box 1017 • Oakland, CA 94604-1017
Call your credit card order to: 800-266-5564
Fax: 510-763-9198